chasing the mouse

Father Nathan Monk

Chasing
the Mouse

Nathan Monk

Copyright © 2015 Nathan Monk

All rights reserved.

www.FatherNathanMonk.com
FatherNathan@gmail.com

ISBN:0692535306
ISBN-13: 9780692535301

Cover design and texts: copyright © 2015 by Tashina Monk
Cover illustration: copyright © 2015 by Aimee Monk

DEDICATION

Above all else, this book is dedicated to my amazing partner in life, Tashina, and our three wonderful children, Kira, Selena, and Gideon. Without your support and our adventures together, this book would have never been possible.

To my amazing parents: Though my life growing up was difficult because of our family's struggle with poverty and homelessness, you worked tirelessly to give us hope and opportunity.

For my dear friend, Sean Dugas: Words will never express how heartbreaking it is that you are no longer here. A small part of me will always know that this book would have been just a little bit better had you been around to fix it.

Finally, this book is dedicated to all children and families who have survived homelessness and those who are currently within its grips. You are not alone and there is hope. No matter what happens, never give up.

❧

ACKNOWLEDGMENTS

*A special thanks to Steve Heneghan, Carl Wernicke, Chip &
Sharon Henderson, Michael Odonovan, Bob Sanders, Meagan M
Parker, and Monica Haviland.*

*A very special thanks to Aimee Monk for turning my family into
cartoons.*

*And of course, true appreciation should be given to the fairy
godparents of Pensacola, Quint and Rishy Studer, not only for
bibbidi bobbidi booing this city back to life, but also for giving me the
opportunity to help make dreams come true.*

CONTENTS

For as long as I can remember I have seen my brother as my hero. There was not a single time I didn't seek out his help, from accidentally cutting my foot on broken glass when I was 9 to asking advice on coming out to my family when I was 19. Not once did I think he wavered in strength and courage. Unfortunately, there were small portions of my life when I turned my back on him. I chose to believe mean and awful things religious people in my life said about him. I didn't take the time to question why these people believed these things about him or what their motives were. At the time, I didn't realize that all along he was fighting for people like me. He has always fought against injustice and gone to extremes to stand up against it. My brother helped mold me with the strength and mercy of a father and the blunt teasing of a brother. More importantly he opened my mind to see people as people. It was my brother who showed me that what others saw as a dirty homeless man on the street was so much more than what put him there. He taught me that a man kissing another man was not sick or wrong—it was just love and it was beautiful. And the more difficult lesson he taught me was that the parents who hurt me are just people figuring it all out too. Now, don't get me wrong, my brother has flaws. I have had many days where I believed I would never speak to him again, only to realize I couldn't call him to tell him about it. I have the privilege of being his little sister. He preceded me and

1

experienced so much of the hurt by himself, and because of those experiences I was able to feel less alone. With every twist in our already bumpy road I knew that he would be around the corner on his horse donned with full armor to save the day. Little did I know, he might've also needed to be saved.

The scars that are left with us from childhood are rarely the fault of any one person. Often times they are just the result of chance and circumstance. The personalities, strengths, and weaknesses of the people who play vital roles in cultivating who we are can be both a great service and a huge detriment and we have no choice in the matter. Despite intentions, the wounds from others are real and have long-term effects. We can grow up and learn more about the details of events that stick out in our hearts and minds, but in the end, facts don't change feelings.

In my own life, I have had the odd experience of what I can only describe as floating through homelessness. I was young enough that staying in motel rooms, bug infested homes, and even the van, didn't seem out of the ordinary. Because I was so young, I never questioned where my father was all day or what he did so that I would be able to eat. Instead, I was content with watching The Little Mermaid for the 100th time on a fuzzy motel television. The only thing on my mind was wishing I could tell Ariel that fathers do in fact reprimand their daughters on land too. At the time, I didn't know why my mother was so sad or why my father didn't seem to ever do anything right. What I did know is that I had a big brother who would spend hours trying to turn my long hair into a wicked mohawk or just listen to my stories as we set in the ruins of our (sort-of) back yard. I was not burdened with knowing that I couldn't be like other kids because Daddy didn't have money. I just thought dad was a jerk but at least I had my big brother. As I have grown older I am now able to understand the seriousness of our poverty and the realities behind it. As these things have become clearer, I realize that my Dad was a good man and my Mom was doing the very best that she could. That doesn't erase the fact that this isn't what it feels like to a child.

In this book, my brother has taken on the challenge of lining up those two contrasting views, looking at the world of poverty both from the vantage point of a child and now as an adult, and I must say he has done it well. He explains with simplicity what it means to be human. The raw truth of what it is to like to feel love and hurt. This book is not really about my brother, my family, or even the mouse we chased for so many years. I believe in my heart that this book is about understanding the human experience no matter what that experience looks like.

ANNA LEIGH MONK

So much of my life has been defined by my tenure as a priest—both during my time in good standing and now my season of separation from the Church. Without a doubt, much of the drama that has defined who I have become as a person was formed in the refining fire of the priesthood. However, before the bishop smeared the oil of blessing over my palms and left its indelible mark, I was just a young boy trying to figure out what life meant. Long before I ever celebrated the mystery of the Eucharist or heard my first confession, I had to deal with the perils of puberty and bifocal glasses.

When I made the decision to step down from the priesthood on that summer day, it left far more questions than answers for many people. Some asked me why I waited so long to come out in support of marriage equality. My support for the LGBTQ community on issues such as adoption or even my notorious counter protests of the anti-gay demonstrators at pride festivals was well documented. For those who knew me as their priest, confessor, and spiritual father, the agony of feeling like they had lost me to the rushing waters of progress left a certain void, and that chasm brought demands to answer their questions of "why?"

I was left to reflect on many of these things myself. How had I come to this point in life where my faith was at odds with the reality that was in front of me? I loved the Church for her beauty and majesty. For the way in which the words of Jesus had echoed for two millennia the mantra of loving your neighbor and being kind to those you had met. However, I was forced by virtue of my conscience to answer within myself how I could reconcile the love of my neighbor, while my religion was demanding that my neighbor could not love whomever they choose.

Many people rightfully asked me to explain how I got to this point within the context of a book. Something tangible that they could read within the confines of their own home to try to understand the process by which I had fallen from grace or come to see the light, depending upon which vantage point they were evaluating my apostasy from.

As I set down to write those pages, I became stuck attempting to explain away my childhood. I would explain away in the simplest of terms about my personal experience with poverty and homelessness as a youth. In a paragraph I would attempt to divulge all of the heartache that came with watching my family fall apart right before my eyes. So I would rework a piece here, add a little more details here, but after a while it seemed that I would never reach the destination of explaining my priesthood and it's shortcomings. My shortcomings.

Then I realized the fundamental flaw. If I were to subtly reference most anything in my life, a person could research it and find the answers. A brief mention about me being arrested while protesting the bible thumpers or the time I was nearly drug out of city hall are all documented events. They are tangible black and white facts that people can see for themselves. They can judge the nature of my perspective of events up against the real life data.

With my childhood this was not the case. I had held so deeply to this great hurt of growing up homeless that I had never truly reconciled it, much less spoken about it publicly. With this came a great inconsistency in my life, that the very thing that motivated me to become a priest, to care for the poor, and fight for the unhoused, was the thing I had spent the least amount of time evaluating.

I suppose I did it in many ways to protect my mother or to maintain a relationship with my father. These were my justifications. I did not need to talk about the horrors I had personally experienced at the hands of a fragile economy in order to try to help others. Talking about my own trauma could distract from the cause or might discredit me. People might think I was too close to the situation, only speaking from a point of emotion. These are the things I convinced myself of. Little did I know I was really struggling with the shame of being shackled with that word, the other indelible mark: Homeless.

What I was able to realize, only after leaving the priesthood, is that it was those years in my youth that truly defined me, not some collar strapped around my neck. It was the education that I received on the streets and in those shady motels that gave me a heart and sympathy for those whom I felt God had called me to serve within my vocation. Their story was my story. When I would rise up and stand in between a police officer and a panhandler on the verge of being arrested, I was not standing up only for this man that I did not know, but I was now an adult finally doing what I was unable to do as a child. That homeless man holding a sign, trapped within a system that improperly handles his mental illness is my mother, my brother, my sisters. He is my father.

As I wrote out the first few chapters of the book I was supposed to be writing, the one about my life as a priest, it became painfully obvious that if I were to tell you the story about how a homeless man named Skunk held a prison shank blade against my throat for inadvertently exposing him as a felon, my lack of fear in that situation did not make sense. I would seem virtually mad, or maybe even a liar to say that in that moment I did not feel fear. I grabbed his wrist and threw him to the ground, and lay there holding him peacefully as I waited for the police to arrive. I may have been a shepherd, but the holy oil the bishop had placed upon my hands had not removed all of the calluses of my youth.

I needed to explain properly that the fear of my life being taken from me was destroyed long before, when, as a seventeen-year-old boy, a man placed a gun in my face in the alley way of a two-bit motel my father had rented. When the man told me to drop to my knees and placed that steel against my nose, I was forced to face my own death. Would he rape me? Was this my last moment on earth? As he released me unharmed after stealing whatever few worldly processions I had left, I ran into the room where my father waited. I screamed obscenities for him to call the police. I was chastised for cursing. Then, in that moment, my life and its value was placed firmly in perspective. Appearances, even in the face of abject poverty, above all things. I learned that lesson.

The juxtaposition of my life, as a child hardened by poverty, and then as an adult trying to address the systematic oppression that forced my childhood to be this way, are issues that had to be addressed before I could explain my priesthood.

This is the beginning of my story, whether or not these pages will have any value for others I do not know. I will be eternally grateful that I went back to this place. That I visited again in my mind these places I lived. The experiences I felt. That I looked at my father again through the raw anger of a teenager, but then baptized him in my mind with seasoned wisdom.

I abandoned the book that others wanted me to write in order to reconcile within myself who I really am and how I got here. This book is not a condemnation of my parents, the Church, or even society. It is just the story of what happened and most importantly what it felt like. Above all this story is about the emotion. Finally being able to confront and exorcise the demons of my childhood has brought about much peace.

NATHAN MONK

chasing the mouse

Father Nathan Monk

Prologue. Once upon a time

*"I only hope that we don't lose sight of one thing -
that it was all started by a mouse."*
-Walt Disney

It is often said that smell has the most powerful memory recall, but I think that sound is pretty compelling as well. There are certain sounds in this world that are so distinctive that they instantly release us into vivid past moments. The sound of a dog panting, the faint blast of an ambulance racing by, the drip of an icicle as winter turns into spring. Throughout my life, there are certain sounds I will never forget. The liberating scream my wife made as our children were delivered. The sobs of the widow sitting in the front row of the little chapel where I officiated my first funeral. When my oldest daughter first called me, "Daddy." These noises can instantly draw us back into thoughts of happiness or drag us deep into all-consuming darkness. I have stood in homeless encampments and watched as a Vietnam War veteran shifted from "normal," but then a clash happens and suddenly he is on the ground engaged again in a rigorous battle of a senseless war. Smells can trigger a memory, but I think sound can often be a time machine, whisking us away into the recesses of our minds where our pain replays in endless loops of repression.

Of all the sounds in this world that illicit recall, few of them stand out as that noxious blast that police officers make when they slam their grinding fists upon a door. I have often mused that there must be an entire class in the Police Academy devoted to this gut wrenching cymbal. No matter how many times I have heard the sound, the piercing knock forever remains the same, as though it is an ancient song passed down from one generation of masters to the next. It does not seem to matter if they are coming to the rescue or if you are a renegade on the run, that knock remains resolute. Powerful. Dramatic. For me, personally, it takes me back to the same place every time. I am a child sitting in a run down, musky motel. Our few remaining essential earthly belongings surround my mother and she is weeping tears with desperate wails. She has finally reached the end of the road. It was those sounds my mother made in concert with the beating fist of the officer, those deafening, thunderous sounds that I hoped to never hear again. As fate would have it, today I often hear this very sound. Sometimes daily. However, my ability to resolve those tears is substantially different from the vantage point, because then I was as a boy without any power or understanding of what was happening to us.

My small hands turned the lock to open the door in response to the officer's demands. His voice echoed with the bang of his hand as it made contact with the metal door, "This is the police. Open up." The door cracked open with a screech. My small frame stood roughly where his badge could stare back directly into my wide, terrified eyes. The short motel owner stood behind him, yelling at my mother the instant the door opened. He was full of fury and hatred, his words deep and poignant, albeit mostly incoherent through his accent. Still, the words that mattered could be heard loud and clear.

Homeless.

Worthless.

Lazy.

These labels attached to our souls like tattoos. Marks that would remain with us like Cain. Each village we would retreat to could see clearly that we were damned. What was the crime worthy of this today? We were thirty minutes over our check out extension and if we did not pay, we had to leave immediately. There were drug dealers six rooms down from us, but it was poverty that was receiving the full length of the law's long arm.

Quickly we loaded everything in the back of the van. My father was attempting to make money so we could stay, but his ambitions failed. Instead, he made arrangements for us to sleep at a friend's house. No explanation for our poverty would be given, only promises that it would one day get better. Dad would desperately try to control the narrative of our homelessness, but it is difficult in such close quarters to keep children from understanding how profound the depth of your poverty truly is. We would shuffle from motels to couches and our van. I cannot estimate how many different motels or locations we lived in, since these things seemed liked trivial exteriors to the circumstance of the reality that resounded in my heart.

We were homeless.

However, even at a young age I was able to understand that my mother was depressed and on medication and my sister needed to see a doctor, but there seemed to be no way to get treatment. The emergency room was the only solution. As attempts were made to run ahead of the quicksand of poverty, it seemed there were always more bills to be paid and never-ending jobs that my father wasn't considered for. We were faced with difficult questions that only crisis can bring: How would we get our mail? Should he pay for the cell phone or food? He needed the phone for a job, so maybe he could just write another bad check for a pizza.

Every night, my siblings and I sat in front of the TV as my parents covertly fought in slightly hushed tones, hiding behind pillows or in shuttered bathrooms as the lime-rusted drains dripped in the background. As times became more desperate, their whispers rose above the commercials and the rustling of guests checking in outside. Just enough reality would seep through the walls and into my own mind to create an unbreakable state of constant fear, but that fear would be crystallized in a thick and murky hatred until suddenly magic filled the room.

My siblings and I watched as a small fairy flew over a castle and everything around us disappeared. In an instant, we were rushed away to fly on magic carpets, run with lions, and dance with kindhearted beasts. For an hour and thirty minutes, paupers were Sultans and peasant girls transformed into princesses with the mere flick of a wrist.

On nights when we slept in the van, I looked at the back of my mother's seat and found a square. Inside that square, I conjured up that same fairy in my innocent mind's eye. She flew over the towers of the castle as I reminded myself that a lovely princess lived inside that castle. Not long before, she was covered in soot and filth, ignored by society. Everything was stacked against her, but she ascended to the top. Maybe these dirty rats scrambling outside the dumpster would transform my own life. Could they be little Jaques in disguise, waiting to whisk us away to a safe and comforting place?

At the end of each classic story, a commercial came on and happy children walked down Main Street, USA, with dads who wore nice suits and moms who smiled. Brothers and sisters played and there was the Mouse, waiting to receive the excited children with loving arms. In reassuring tones Dad would tell us, "As soon as things get better, I will take you." As we would move from a motel to someone's couch and eventually into an abandoned house, my brother and I would replay those classic commercials, "Timmy! It's like no place you've been in your whole life!" And we would pack our suitcases. The imagination was enough. For a while.

As a teenager, the reality began to set in that our family would not go to Disney World. However, that realization was less about the vacation, and more about the reality that the fantasy represented. Life was not going to get better and we were not going to rise above the gutters. At first, it was less about the Mouse and more about getting away from the rats feasting off of our despair. As that realization slowly set in, I became bitter and angry. My feelings grew from a seed of doubt into a monstrous tree of discontentment. I resented my father and I pitied my mother. Those feelings continued to mount as our displacement was patronized with false hope in religious leaders who cared more about their own benefit than fixing the systemic issues related to our poverty. Money could always be found to tithe or to travel to hear prophets. I remember driving with my mother to Orlando to hear the "Word of God." There we were —fifteen minutes away from the magic I was promised—but dollar bills were shimmied over our desperate hands into offering plates as we hoped that prosperity would finally come our way.

What started as a simple childhood hope for a better future soon evolved into an obsession with chasing the mouse. But, it would also cultivate a more productive passion within me. An attempt to create a world where children did not have to grow up as I did. It was a desire that would ultimately lead me in many different directions. In that restless attempt to stop the cycle of poverty that infected my childhood, I would make attempts to fix my family and the flaws I saw within my religion. It would lead me into confrontations with my local government and powerful religious figures. It would elevate me to moments that felt like fame and it would break me to the point of such pain that I would cry out to a God that I wasn't quite certain was listening. However, it would not be until I realized that the only person I could truly fix was myself, and through that, everything would magically fall into place.

Regardless of the success I have achieved in my battles for the rights of the poor and disfranchised, I am always reminded of the villains and heroes that helped me get here. Retrospective thinking has sometimes caused me to realize that I have mistakenly labeled the villains and the heroes. It took a great deal of eye opening moments for me to realize that in this life, we have all—at some point —been villains and heroes. We have all played sidekick, ensemble, and leading roles. The journey hasn't been easy, but as I learned more about the man behind the mouse, I realized it was never promised that it would be easy. There are always witches and evil stepmothers waiting to steal your joy, but if you look hard enough, there are also fairy godmothers in disguise, waiting to show up at just the right moment. Some people throughout the experiment of my own life have seen me as the villain, others as prince charming saving the day. I'm not so sure any of that is fair. At the end of the day I have always remained one thing.

A diamond in the rough.

1. The Circle Of Life

"Why worry? If you've done the very best you can, worrying won't make it any better." -Walt Disney

One Jump Ahead

There are many oddities that accompany the human experience, like the necessity of using the restroom or food as a requirement to survival, but of all the bizarre quirks of this thing we call life, one of the cruelest is the true helplessness of childhood. Whether life has given you abject poverty or the ability to live in a palace, the genuine sense of complete lack of control that we experience in childhood can create extreme levels of anxiety. Many childhood psychiatrists now hypothesize that a toddler's tantrum is the literal result of lack of control and the explosive feeling of being unheard. It certainly makes sense. As a toddler, you are only a couple feet tall, can't perfectly articulate your points, and your parents make all of life's decisions while you simply have to go along with it. You have no choice whatsoever and there is no escape. If parents decide to move across the county or get divorced, those are adult decisions, and as my father often reminded me, "This family is not a democracy." These truths are nearly incomprehensible to the mind of a child. You instinctively know that your parents will take care of you, but as a kid you can't differentiate between the need of food and the want of an action figure. So, you are left to argue about how parents should love each other forever or that they can't move across the country for a better job because you have friends. It seems that the world is perpetually on the parent's side and worse, the universe moves forward without a care or concern for your feelings on the matter. Judges sign papers and dissolve marriages. Moving trucks arrive to take you across country and you are told it is for the greater good.

As an adult, we have no choice but to look back on the childhood moments that we now resent and baptize them in the supposedly rational mind of maturity. We begin to find logic in the actions of our parents—or other "grown-ups"—nodding our heads and saying that we understand their reasoning. I have certainly experienced this in my own life, but I am also sometimes forced to ask the question of who is wiser? My seven-year-old self or my current self? When I find myself now in disciplinary situations or making difficult life altering decisions, I begin to exonerate my parents, but somewhere deep inside me the child version of myself acts as defense attorney for my own kids, because I remember so vividly how horrible that gut wrenching lack of control can feel.

Being a parent now, I know that I have done things that my children will not understand. Someday they may write a book similar to this one about their struggles and hurts. That is the reality of being a parent. You have to make decisions and live with the consequences of those actions, hoping that what you do is for the best, knowing you tried your hardest to do what is right with your space in this world.

When it comes to the earliest years of my own life and my attempt to piece them together, I realized that I would only be able to tell those stories from the limited view of a child. There was so much information I was not given, details that are overlooked by my own adolescent ignorance or the pure selfishness of childhood. So many angles that I simply could not see from my highly limited stature. Standing here now—from the higher, but not necessary better vantage point of adulthood—I know that my parents loved my siblings and me. They truly tried to give us what we needed, while at the same time seeking after their own ambitions. It is easy as a child to view these actions as parents being selfish, but in many cases that probably comes from childhood narcissism. You want everything and you are told that the world is fresh and new, that you can have anything. It is not true, but you believe it anyway. When your parents fail in some capacity, that hurt is deep. After all, you are only guilty of believing in the product of hope that they sell you.

The memories of my youngest years are few. They are flickers of an existence as I tried to discover the planet and my responsibilities were limited. My brain is placing together a billion connections.

This is what love feels like.

This is fire! Don't touch that again, it hurt.

Crying gets attention. That attention is negative.

Smiles are important and make people happy.

But there were also experiences that made impressions that translated into more robust memories. Riding on the back seat of my mother's bike and wondering how the moon seemed to follow us. I know that we talked about it. I know she explained it to me, but I don't remember her words. Only the feelings. The emotions are so strong, even if the direct lesson never penetrated far enough to remain. Other memories are surrounded by the sadness and grief of life, like when a kid my age died and I saw his mother at the grocery store. I wanted to go and talk to her. I told my mother that I needed to go tell her that her son was dead. I do not know to this day what, in my childish mind, made me feel that she wouldn't know or that I should be the one to explain it to her, but I remember my mother gently instructing me away from my innocent foolishness. Again, I don't recall the exact words she used to dissuade me, but the emotion of that experience is still strong enough to remain with me forever.

I do not know why we left our home in DeRidder, Louisiana to move to Nashville, Tennessee. At least I do not believe I did as a child. Now, I know the details that my parents have shared with me during my teenage years or when I have asked questions, trying to piece together my own identity. Sometimes, their reality clashes with my memories. Other times, it connects pieces that were missing.

There is a clear feeling of standing next to a For Sale sign. This is my last memory in Louisiana. I am there in the yard of my mother's dream home. The one that my father had built for her. I imagine that this feeling that the home was supposed to last forever crept in from my mother's emotions over the years and attached itself to this moment. There was a woman standing there with us. She must have been the realtor. But then again, that is my adult mind placing context, trying to justify actions to the confused child that lives inside my mind, perpetually stuck in that moment of complete powerlessness.

ZERO TO HERO

The week we opened our shelter for families, I was driving my oldest daughter to the mall to collect a few things for the Christmas holiday. She wanted to make a present for her mother. Suddenly, I found myself slamming on the breaks. Cars were in pieces directly in front of me. All I could see were tiny little feet coming from underneath one of the vehicles. Though we were a thirty-second walk from the hospital, no emergency responders had arrived on the scene yet. I quickly pulled my car into a vacant parking lot, turned my head around and looked at Kira. "Whatever you do, do not get out of this car. Do not look at anything. Just read your book."

Before she could respond, I was gone. A large crowd of unhelpful bystanders stared in disbelief. A car crashed into a family attempting to cross the road. They hit the mother and her three-year-old daughter. The other three children screamed from across the street. Everyone was in a state of panic. Out of nowhere, doctors arrived and began attending to the wounded. They didn't seem to be moving. It looked like hope was probably lost and the children's screams continued to break the silence of the somber moment.

I walked over to them and one of the children grabbed me. As I looked down at her she begged me, "Please, please don't let my mommy die! She's a good mommy, mister. She's such a good mommy and I love her. She reads to me every night and she loves me. Please, tell Jesus not to let my mommy die."

Those words ripped my heart out of my chest and left it bleeding on the cement. There was absolutely no way I could make that promise. I wasn't so certain that Jesus was listening to my prayers these days anyway. In fact, I was becoming convinced that he blocked my number. I looked over at the mother and sister's lifeless bodies as paramedics attempted to restore life. Police officers moved crowds, roping off the scene. I silently said a prayer in my own soul. I couldn't help it. It was a guttural reaction, almost like an instinct. I pleaded, but I made no promises. Just listened. I set the children down and listened to their story. They were living in a halfway house for women involved in domestic violence. Life wasn't easy and it was about to get a whole lot harder.

I waited with the children until their grandparents arrived. They hugged me and walked away. It was now time for me to return to my vehicle, back to my own child. Kira was crying. She told me she was scared and all she wanted to do was to go home. She was angry with me for stopping. She just wanted to be anywhere other than here, around the fear and dreadful screams.

There will come a day in my life where I know I will have to answer to my daughter for my choice to stop the car that day. I could have easily been like a hundred other cars that rubbernecked their way past the scene, but that just isn't me. I had to go with my conscience and everything inside my being told me that those children needed someone there. Not someone who would make promises they couldn't keep or make them on behalf of a deity, but someone who could help reduce the fear. However, I purchased that release for those kids at the expense of my own daughter's comfort. Did I make the right choice? It felt right in the moment. I know I did something important for some, harmful to others. Does the good outweigh the bad? That is the burden of choices. It's likely that I will never know.

What I did learn in that moment is that no matter what a parent puts a child through, whether it is homelessness, having an abusive spouse, or trying to be a hero, the children do know that their parent's are good, that they love them, and read them stories. I know it about my own mother and father. And I hope my children will one day see it in me.

HAKUNA MATATA

The beginning of my childhood in Nashville was arguably one of the more pleasurable times of my life. My brother and I lived in a propaganda film for free-range parenting. We were homeschooled, lived on farms, traveled down creeks, and battled serpents. We built forts in the summer and had snowball fights in the winter. I tried my hand at falling in love for the first time with the freckled redhead girl with a perpetually broken arm.

She lived just down the street and we spent time riding horses and living out the stories of Tom and Huck. I even shot a robin and killed it. I remember watching it lie in the snow, it's blood trickling out, staining the pure white around it. I vowed to never pick up a gun again. These were experiences, moments trapped in time, and they are good times that last forever. I often visit these places in my mind. Watching my sister Emily fall out of the barn window as she replayed a scene from the Princesses Bride, hoping my brother would catch her. He didn't. So, a trip to the hospital quickly followed. I recount these times over and again in my mind, hoping that these will overshadow the trauma that waited on the other side for us all. For in a brief moment, the house and dreams found within it would all come crashing down.

The uncertainty of childhood is another cruel part of the human experience. When you are an adult, you begin to build up certain expectations based upon life experience. As a child, you do not have this ability because everything is new. No promise has ever been broken. When you are an adult, you begin to understand the rhythm of life, or at least become cynical, and you start to notice the patterns. You learn these lessons and begin to avoid familiar pitfalls and dangers. However, when you are kid you truly believe that the bicycle rigged with umbrellas and the sheets from your parent's bed will fly off the roof, or that the clock you took apart will absolutely transport you back in time. As an adult, you know that is not true. If time travel were real, hopefully someone would have fixed this mess by now. But then again, maybe not. They are probably sitting on a deserted island. Hiding.

In those first and earliest years of my life, I had no idea about the coming tragedies that awaited our family. Surely, I experienced mild hurts and traumas. My father lied to me, even if he wouldn't define it that way. I'm certain he didn't mean to, but he did make empty promises. That is just a fact, not a condemnation. I remember early on feeling that my younger brother was favored over me. But these are not abnormal feelings. This is part of growing up and the danger of relying too much on perspective. Could my parents have been better at raising us? I don't know that is a fair question to even entertain. Humans are always evolving, inventing, discovering, but within the family unit that happens in the micro. How can a parent truly know how to raise children when we are all pulling from broken pieces of our own upbringing and those things we've seen around us, on TV, in films, or read in books? My parents tried. That is far better than other parents can claim. They were present and that is light-years beyond parents who abandon their kids for other lives or drugs. In this sense, my parents were perfect.

At the end of the day, my mommy read to me and I know she loved me. But that does not change the reality of what happens next, nor does what happens next define my parents as people. It is just, quite simply, what happened next.

2. A Dream is a Wish Your Heart Makes

"I'd say it's been my biggest problem all my life... it's money. It takes a lot of money to make these dreams come true." -Walt Disney

THE SANTA CLAUS

We weren't born poor. Once upon a time, life was happy and normal. I was a privileged white kid from the south. Now, I don't mean to misrepresent our social or economic status. Our family wasn't wealthy, but we were definitely alright. The 80's were a mythical time where the average middle class American family could afford two cars, a house, and childcare. It was a land before cell phones and computers that followed us everywhere. Dads got off of work at 5PM and emails weren't following him. Only really important dads had pagers that could whisk them away, and my dad didn't have a pager. It was still somewhat the norm for moms to stay at home. In this sense, our family was normal, at least by the median income standards, but after the move, once we actually arrived in Nashville, life instantly became very far removed from the idea of normal.

I clearly remember the day I stopped believing in Santa Clause, almost as clearly as the day I started believing in him again. Life is full of moments that cause us to lose faith in ourselves, others, and humanity. Sometimes, I have abundant faith in a god, but other moments level my faith in such a creator to being little more than that of, "If one exists, that god must be mean." It seems that when I dive down into those moments of absolute despair, something miraculous happens. Of course, then I watch a Penn and Teller video of a magician performing far more spectacular things than I've ever seen a god do and I wonder again.

The moments that I believe in a Deity the most is around the holidays. Not simply because it feels very lonely to be atheistic during Jesus' birthday, but mostly because people are so damn good during the Christmas season. They give more, spend more time with family, and try so hard to make other people's lives better. It has been lamented in works far greater than my own, that it would be wonderful if people could keep the spirit of Christmas all year round. Unfortunately, in the south the only part of the Christmas spirit that lingers all yearlong are holiday lights on double wides.

My faith in good ol' Saint Nick came crashing to a climatic halt the day that he knocked on my door.

Imagine the surprise of my brother and I as we approached our windowed front door to the apartment, only to find Santa standing right there waiving at us, five whole weeks before Christmas. With a ho-ho-ho, he grabbed his belly with a jolly-ish wave. This Santa seemed less than stellar upon closer inspection. Not only did he lack a certain magical quality necessary to canvas the entire planet in an evening, but his beard looked fake. Once he entered the home, it became clear that this Bishop of Myra was an absolute bullshit fraud. It was my father.

This was far from a Tim Allen movie. My father had not mystically transformed into the actual Santa Clause, thus bringing joy and happiness to children all across the globe. He was instead making minimum wage as an inauthentic replica of the Coca-Cola saint at a local grand hotel. Our next door neighbor had connections at the place and secured my father the job. This is the first memory I have of our descent from normalcy. I doubt that at the young age of seven I was able to comprehend that my father working some Miracles on 34th Street meant that we were poor. But I certainly grasped that no one would be coming down our chimney. Mostly because we didn't have one and secondly because my dad wasn't really Santa. Little did I know then, one day the real Santa would visit our home to make up for all this mess.

The first week the shelter opened, I received a call from a panic-stricken woman. She had just been released from jail and to say that her mother had been irresponsible in taking care of her children would be an understatement. The children had not been taken to school regularly and their social security cards and birth certificates were missing. The young mother decided to move in with some friends for a few weeks while she sought employment, because her arrest led to her losing her job, car, and nearly her children. One simple mistake of association turned her life upside down.

I received the call during dinner with my family and left abruptly. For the average family, this may have been something unusual, unless maybe your dad was a surgeon or something. However, after spending nearly a decade as a priest, my family was plenty well accustomed to me leaving at the drop of a hat. Outside of working as a parish priest, I had also been a part-time chaplain at a funeral home. For me, leaving at a moment's notice was the name of the game. I was constantly rushing away to give Last Rites or to be at a crash site with a grieving family. Now, my newly found vocation operating a cold night shelter for families proved to provide equal levels of unstable schedules and excitement.

As I took a right and then a left into a forgotten area of town—only referenced occasionally on the evening news—it was clear I was the only white person to have intentionally turned onto these streets in a long time. This suspicion of mine was confirmed after finally arriving at my destination. When I knocked on the front door, a small child with an adult-sized scowl greeted me. It was very similar to the suspicious looks I received on the drive over.

"You a cop?" he questioned.

"No," I said. "I am not a cop."

"Are you from the state? You going to take us away?"

"No, I am not from the state. But I am here to take you and your mom with me. I have a big house downtown where you can stay for a while."

"Ok, but are you sure you aren't a cop? You look like a cop."

After slowly gaining this young man's trust, I was cautiously welcomed into the home. The toilet was broken and only one or two lights worked. The woman who lived there began defending herself. She assured me that she really wasn't cold hearted. She was already taking care of her grandchildren and her own daughter. She had taken in this family for a few weeks and there was just simply not enough room or food for everyone. I could also sense a fear that this family's presence was drawing attention to certain government officials, most notably the Department of Children and Families. This grandmother was not willing to let her grandchildren be drawn into an investigation because of someone else's life choices. I couldn't fault her for that.

We loaded everyone into the van and made our way to the shelter. It had only been open a week or so and business had not yet picked up. The kids picked the largest room and began to unpack. One of the daughters found a package amongst some of the donations that had recently been dropped off. It was a medium-sized pink box. Inside it contained a small Made in China tea set embossed with the images of Disney characters.

"Mister, can I have this?" she asked.

Her mother looked up at me, mortified. There were so many more important things to ask from me. They immediately needed shelter and food. Mom needed to find a job. Careless things like toys were not necessary in a crisis and to say that they were a luxury would have been an understatement. I gave the mother a reassuring glance and told her it was all right, "This is what these toys are here for." Of course, that wasn't an entirely accurate statement. They had been given to the shelter as Christmas presents and we were still many weeks away from the holiday, but I figured this might be the closest thing to Christmas these kids would see. Once I gave my approval for them to have the gift, the two sisters tore into the box and pretended to have a tea party.

The youngest sister asked one of the brothers if he would play tea party with them. He quickly made a disgusted face and explained how he's not a girl and wouldn't play a girl's game.

"Well, you know tea parties need gentlemen as well," I explained to him.

The sisters quickly chimed in that he should be a gentleman and join them. He seemed skeptical. I sat down and began to sip away at the imaginary beverage in our glasses. After a while, he joined us. His older brother was in the corner drawing and he came to join us as well. He began to explain to me how much he loved to draw.

"You know," he said. "I hear that Disney has a lot of drawing jobs. One day, I think I will move to Disney World and be a drawer. Then I will be able to take care of my mom. It will be like a vacation every day. I'm gonna ask Santa to bring me some drawing stuff for Christmas. Do you believe in Santa and magic and stuff like that?"

I paused for a moment to reflect upon my own childhood. Sitting before me were children who lived a very similar life to my own, but in many ways so very different. Though my father choosing to be Santa that holiday season destroyed my belief in that myth, I also had a father who was willing to put on a red suit to put food on our table, something this family was noticeably lacking. Although my thoughts of Santa had been dashed upon the rocks of necessity and survival, later in life I would be given the opportunity to believe again. It was upon that story that I formed the answer to this innocent question.

"You know, when I was a kid, my parents didn't have a lot, and once we were sort of squatting in a house. I didn't know what was going to happen, and I knew my parents didn't have any money. We went to bed that Christmas Eve with nothing, but the next morning our tree was filled with everything we could have wanted. Not just toys, but food and blankets, everything. Everything my brothers and sisters had hoped for and more. It was all there. I don't know who brought it. I just know it wasn't my parents. I think there is only one explanation."

"Santa!" he shouted. He was a little too old to really believe anymore, but sometimes we all need a little delusion to survive another day.

That day, I had gone from being a scary cop to the Mad Hatter leading a tea party, with pirates and princesses living in perfect harmony. I cried the entire way home.

WALKING THE PLANK

Looking back, now as an adult, it is easy to see the missteps that my father made that slowly walked our family off into poverty, but I think that hindsight is a cruel mistress and to borrow a phrase of my partner, Tashina, it is very "victim blame-y." The reality is, if we could know the outcomes of all of our decisions, we would likely not make those mistakes or we would just sit in the corner of our room rocking back and forth crippled with fear. I will not attempt to make this into a commentary on how my dad could have prevented what happened. Far too many people in our life, at that time, were quick to make those accusations.

Once, a friend of my father's attempted to sell him on joining him in a stock venture. Because of my dad's personal feelings on the stock market and his contention that it was akin to gambling—a steady no-no to a recovering Baptist—he refused. Needless to say, his friend purchased stock in a start up Internet company that rhymes with oogle, and does not have to worry about much anymore these days. Many other business decisions that failed came and went as my father pursued his personal dream/addiction of being a musician. In many ways, these ventures became distractions to that dream. His risks became higher as each seeming failure became more baggage to carry. The next venture had to assume the cost of the latter experiment. He would take a minister of music position that he didn't love in order to pay off the debt of the antique store that didn't work. He would do this just long enough to purchase his Create-a-Book franchise that was supposed to pay for itself and give him extra money in order to produce an album. The album would be put on the back burner because he was too busy doing session voice work for someone else's record in order to quickly pay the second mortgage that funded the book business. And that's why the old lady swallowed the spider to catch the fly. Maybe he wasn't as opposed to gambling after all.

My father purchased a log house on a hill that overlooked a small creek. My fondest memories of my childhood reside in this home. If I am honest with myself, it is the last place during my childhood that felt like an actual home. Everything else beyond this point gave the sense that we were refugees in flight.

I was an awkward youth, wearing big bifocal glasses to correct a lazy eye, and it was during these years in this home that I was diagnosed with dyslexia. I was told that I would never read or write beyond a second grade level. However, I would like to think that I have far exceeded that dire diagnosis in these first few chapters. It would be to the credit of my mother that I moved beyond that damning sentence. She was a former special education teacher who decided to step out of the work force to help raise us and was a homeschooling advocate. It was a very hard day for her when she finally admitted that it might be best for me to enter into public school to receive extra training to overcome my disability.

These things are the privilege of the middle class. Mothers or fathers choosing to stay home to attend to their children and the ability to fight for those children. Far later in life I would see first hand, as a professional working in the area of poverty, how many parents are required to forfeit this type of advocacy for their children. Many others will make great sacrifices for their children that will lead them into homelessness.

Soon, my siblings and I would be homeschooling again, this time not for any ideological reasons, but because it would become too difficult to keep us in school with the instability that would become our life. It is hard to keep kids in school while you are living in motels and minivans parked outside of Walmart, staying up all night and hoping that security doesn't run you off as your groggy parents slowly drive from one parking lot to the next.

During the last winter in our log home upon the hill, we would not know those fears. My brother would help me build an igloo and we would slide down the ice driveway on trash can tops. As winter melted into spring, we camped on our lawn and made stew out of the craw-daddies we caught from the creek, neither of us willing to admit how disgusting our concoction of rice and freshwater shellfish living off of god-knows-what-sludge was.

These years felt very much life the American dream, but they would soon collide with the hidden American reality.

3. God Help the Outcasts

"I always like to look on the optimistic side of life,
but I am realistic enough to know that life is a complex
matter." -Walt Disney

One Step Ahead of the Breadline

A common misconception concerning homelessness is that it is a sudden occurrence. Obviously there are certain cases when this does happen. Over the last decade of social justice work, I have seen flash homelessness occur. People lose their home due to natural disasters, slum lords, or corrupt banking systems. The difference between these sudden emergency homelessness cases and other types of homelessness is the added element of poverty. I was once involved in a forum discussing the effects of homelessness and a woman explained how her family found themselves suddenly homeless for two weeks due to a housing deal that fell apart. They had sold their home and secured the loan for the new home, but something fell though. They moved into a temporary monthly apartment until a new house could be found within their loan criteria. Many people scoffed at this situation and rightfully so. It certainly does not fit the definition of genuine homelessness, though I am sure the experience was very upsetting and scary for them at the time.

Homelessness sneaks up on you. It stalks you like a malicious predator, constantly lurking over your shoulder waiting for your moment of weakness to finally show though, and then in a sudden moment, it grabs you by the throat and pulls you to the ground. It happens with payment arrangements made on utilities because you had to pay for an emergency or you just pushed something back because you wanted to get your children presents for Christmas. Next thing you know, you are behind on utilities and then rent. Maybe you lost a job and by the time you found your next opportunity, it's been nearly a month and a half, and on top of that, you took a dollar less than you were making at your previous employment. Soon you are shuffling between service agencies begging for help. Your self-esteem is slowly eaten away by the same predator that chased you into this corner. You are the gazelle that stopped by the watering hole unaware that the crocodile was hiding right below the surface.

I think the first time I began to realize that things were not okay was when I went grocery shopping with my mother. I had wanted ravioli and there was a specific brand I was particularly fond of. My mother had avoided taking me and my siblings grocery shopping for a few months. The house that had become our home was no longer ours. I do not know if it was foreclosed or if it was sold for what was owed or maybe a little below. Those are all common narratives I hear now. My adult brain can only make assumptions as to what realities my parents faced. We had moved into a smaller place further away from town. I do not remember what my father was doing for work at the time. I do know that things seemed on edge. One day, my brother and I were doing target practice with my BB gun and accidentally shot one of the windows. I should have kept my vow. My father was furious with us. Nothing was said about the potential dangers we had presented to our family by our stupidity of shooting toward the house, only the potential cost of the window was mentioned.

When my mother and I arrived at the grocery store, a friendly man who was tasked with returning the carts back to their place greeted us. He always wore a ten-gallon hat and smiled at everyone who walked by. It was my favorite part of going to the grocers. We rushed inside and Mom began making practical selections—eggs, cheese, bread, milk. I wandered up and down the frozen food section perusing a large selection of overly processed "Italian" foods. Near the middle lay my prized ravioli. I picked one out and began to make my way back toward my mom, when suddenly my eye caught the symbols at the end of one of the aisles. I was nearly twelve and I was still unable to read, but any child in their right mind knew the advertised emblems of their favorite delicacies. There, on the frozen food end cap, sparkled a special prized item my young heart could hardly resist. Haagen Dazs bars. I could not remember the last time I had tasted one of these delicious chocolate and almond-covered goodies. I picked out a box and carried my wares in tote, slyly placing them in the cart unnoticed.

The time had come to check out and I was beyond ready. My only care in the world was whether or not my scrumptious foods would melt on the long drive back to our rental. Then everything changed very suddenly. The cashier seemed especially annoyed. I picked up on that pretty quickly and my mother seemed concerned. Without warning, the cashier picked up the phone next to the register and pushed a button.

"We need manager assistance with Food Stamps."

She said it while staring at my mother, almost as if it was intentional. When I was a kid, food stamps did not operate using a subtle EBT debit card that can easily be concealed. No, they were dollar bill styled notes with a certain value attributed to each one. It was a complicated and confusing system that often led to embarrassing moments just like this. I did not know that we were on food stamps. I doubt I really even knew what food stamps were, but I was about to learn a great deal about the stigma that surrounded one of the highest symbols of poverty in America.

My mother began to quickly fumble through her purse. I do not know what she was looking for or if she was really even looking for something at all. Before the manager arrived, I noticed that the line behind us was growing ever longer. A woman began to survey our wares lining the belt, still waiting to be bagged. The Haagen Dazs ice cream that I had coveted apparently stood out like a sign of decadence for which we were clearly unworthy.

"Well, I hope they enjoy the ice cream I just bought them," the woman muttered to herself. Tears flowed from my mother's eyes. Everything moved quickly and in slow motion all at once. We made it out to the car and I looked out the window as she wept. It was one of the longest drives home I've ever experienced.

Tuppence a Bag

Stacey called me every few days, mostly because she wanted someone to talk to. She informed me of every detail of her life in short snippets. One of the most memorable stories I endured was the extreme detail she revealed about an abscess tooth and the horrifying make-shift dental work she had to perform on herself in order to drain it. She had been married and her husband finally decided that she was simply too much baggage to carry along during his struggle with poverty. He abandoned her and left her to fend for herself as a woman living on the streets. She survived off of canned meats and beans. Anything else she needed, she would head to the street corners and hold a small hand written cardboard sign to beg for help.

The county had recently made it illegal for people to panhandle along certain intersections and highways. For years, I had fought diligently to prevent these ordinances from moving forward. A few years before, Tashina and I had been driving along a popular roadway and noticed a man holding a sign begging for help. His wife and young daughters were sitting behind him on a bus stop bench. I pulled over and offered for him to go eat at a restaurant nearby. However, the father informed me that he couldn't leave his post because he needed a few extra dollars in order to be able to stay in a motel room. I wondered in that moment if my own father had ever stood on the side of the road like this. I demanded that he go eat with his family and told him that I would be glad to hold his sign for him instead. It must have been quite the sight to see a priest standing there on the side of the road holding a large cardboard sign which read, "Help Me Feed My Starving Family." Little did I know, that moment would change me forever.

Shortly after that experience, the county began its campaign to make this activity illegal. I saw firsthand how this ability to beg for help spared this family from sleeping in their car or on the streets. It purchased them just one more night in a motel. How many families would suffer the fear of being thrown out of their nightly rentals, just like I had experienced in my own youth, if this was made illegal? How many mothers would turn to prostitution or stealing formula off the shelves, if this safety net of simply asking for help from your fellow man was made into a crime with equal punishment as theft or solicitation?

After the first round of the criminalization of panhandling passed, I dreaded who would be the first to be arrested. I did not have to wait long for the query to be answered. Shortly after enforcement began, I received a call in the middle of the night.

"Father Nate."

I instantly recognized the voice. It was Stacey. She explained how she had been arrested earlier that afternoon. She needed tampons and nowhere in town supplied them. She had been sitting in a holding cell for hours, bleeding down her leg, trying desperately to remember my number. One bail bondsman after another turned her away because she was homeless. However, one of them knew of me and found my number and gave it to her. She frantically gave me all of this information. She needed about a hundred dollars to make bail and also to find a bail bondsman who would post it. I looked at the clock. It was nearly 1AM. Where in the hell was I going to find someone who could help with $100 bucks in the middle of the night?

There was only one person I could think of that operated a business that late. A few years before, I met a strip club owner who was very involved in the social activism scene. We had become a unique odd couple—a priest and the Madame of Pensacola. I sent her a quick text message explaining the story. A few moments later I received a response.

"It's at the club in an envelope. Ryan has it."

Now for a bondsman. In hurried motions I put on my suit and clerical collar and swung by the strip club. I quickly began to debate what would appear more scandalous, a priest walking into a strip club with his collar on or off. I opted to keep it on, because at least no one could accuse me of trying to hide my activities. I couldn't help but feel the irony that I was probably the only man in history who was leaving this establishment with more money than he had walked in with.

I pulled into the first bail bondsman's office I could find and gave it my best smile.

"Jesus Christ," he said, shaking his head. "Let me guess, you are some Mother Teresa style do gooder here about that homeless lady."

I nodded in affirmation. It seemed like this entire situation was moving in my favor and would be best if I just let this thing play out.

"Damn it all, Padre. She was persistent, but I didn't know she would be sending the God-squad in here."

Within a few hours, he was writing her bond and her bail was posted. In the late hours of the night, they finally let her go. She looked cold and tired as the rain began to drip down on our faces. She got in the car, seemingly scared and ashamed. Finally, she broke the silence.

"Pastor, ain't nobody still got me any tampons."

The more I became exposed to our poverty, a bitterness began to grow inside me. I started to truly resent my father. He had taken a menial part time job and our family was now living in a small one-room shack at the top of a winding road right outside of town. How this place was even considered habitable was beyond me. There was a Sonic Drive-In at the bottom of the road, across the street. My brother and I would walk around the streets collecting change. Every few weeks we would collect enough to split a hot dog or slushy.

My responsibilities at home began to grow as my mother's health deteriorated. Years of poverty and undiagnosed illnesses had begun to weigh upon her mind. Her weight had become an issue and her mental stability was waning. Most days she spent sitting in our family mini-van in the slanted driveway talking to her sisters or other folks taking on the charge of makeshift therapist. Most people were recommending that she leave my father, but she refused.

Religion had always been a part of our lives growing up. I wouldn't say that there was ever a time where we lacked a system of faith, but as my father found it more difficult to explain our plight, we also stopped attending any services regularly. After a few years of this, my mother took the reins and we began regular services again. In all honesty, it was a wonderful escape. At youth group on Wednesday nights we did not discuss these types of things. We were all too busy with the spectacular music, worrying about girls, and debating theology

50

to care about our parents. Of course, it was constantly on my own mind, but I did not share it with my friends.

It was a medium-sized charismatic evangelical congregation in the vein of Jesus Camp. I did not want to fall over or pretend to speak in tongues, but soon it seemed like a small price to pay for acceptance with a peer group. I had been living in a type of isolation that was nearly unbearable, constantly taking care of siblings, cooking dinners, and changing diapers. When I was not attending to them, I was attending to my mother.

Some nights, I skipped youth group and walked a few blocks down to the local cinema. I became quite the professional at sneaking into the movies, grabbing empty large pop corn containers and soda cups, and taking them up to the concession stand to cash in on the free refills that were only permitted for those who had actually purchased these items. I would hide from my parents and Jesus, choosing instead to be whisked away to another world, because outside there was far too much reality. My teen years were diminishing and I was afraid that if something didn't change soon, I wouldn't be allowed back into Narnia.

"A man should never neglect his family for business."- Walt Disney

MOTHER KNOWS BEST

I've attempted to accurately chronicle the timeline of events between houses and motels to no avail. I have estimated that we lived in some forty different locations, maybe more, during our time in Nashville. It is difficult to remember when we were staying in motels, houses, couch surfing, or sleeping in our van in a supermarket parking lot. It's also nearly impossible to discern which events took place where. It all seems to blur together. Attempting to dismantle everything and make sense of it always seems to drag me back into a darkness I have desperately tried to suppress. For the sake of my own emotional and mental stability, I will not try to force this madness into a neat chronological series of events. It would be nearly impossible.

What I can state without fear or hesitation is how it all felt. Life became a whirlwind of almosts and promises that weren't kept. In many ways my life was becoming better. While in public school, I had a major breakthrough in my dyslexia and slowly began to develop the ability to read and write. I was enrolled in a typing program and it was like the pieces all began to fall into place. Soon, I was able to read books and keep a journal. However, the struggle of our family poverty was a constant impediment to my personal growth. I was trapped as a teenager with adult responsibilities and anxieties. Were the bills paid? Did the kids have enough to eat?

During this time of constantly hopping from one place to another, I began to vocalize my perceived feelings of my father's failures. Our relationship was already contentious in many ways, mostly because of his vocalized feelings of my own failures. Funny how life works like that. One of my father's greatest flaws is that he is meek and soft spoken to the point that he would continually allow himself to be taken advantage of. In what must have been an unconscious rebellion, I took a different approach to life altogether. I had to be strong and push forward. I would make my own way in this life and nothing would stand in my way. No disabilities or disadvantages would be passed onto me by my parent's choices. There was a world out there and I would leave my mark. If I saw an injustice I would speak out against it. My dad, however, would choose not to make waves. If he saw something he disagreed with, he would choose the path of least resistance, whereas I would force conflict to rise to the top. All wrongdoing must be brought to the surface and confronted.

For this reason, my siblings and mother began to rely on me for things far above the pay grade of a child who was just trying to survive. When my sister would scrape her knee, she would come to me to make the appropriate repairs. If my mother found herself in the throws of her depression, I became the therapist who would sit on the end of her bed and listen to her cry away the pain she felt. This was a minor foreshadowing of the countless confessions I would later hear in my life as a parish priest.

Sometime between leaving our shack on the winding road and many stints in motels, my father found a house in a valley next to a large magnificent horse stable that was no longer in use and had suffered much disrepair. Someone had acquired the massive acreage for some future development, but the house and stable were constantly being broken into. Some kids had even used it for some form of occult practices at some point. When we moved in, there were candles, remnants of incense sticks, and a large pentacle drawn out with red spray paint. This would become our new house.

My father created an arrangement where we would live in the house as a type of watchdog operation until those who owned the land decided to finally develop it. To my father this seemed like a supernatural response. God was clearly looking out for us. I was less certain, but then again He allowed his son to be born in a barn, I'm not sure what I expected Him to put us in.

It was in this not-home that my mother became pregnant with my fourth sibling, bringing the number of kids up to five. I was nearly sixteen years old and I clearly remember the day my parents sat down to tell me.

Mom and Dad sat at the complete opposite ends of the sectional couch that was donated to us. The divide was very telling. Mom cried and Dad smiled slightly. They told me they had news. Part of me wondered if the long run of their marriage had finally reached its end. I would be lying if I denied that part of me had hoped for that. Something made me believe that maybe a slap of reality might force my dad to pull it all together.

The news came that they were pregnant. My mother was pregnant at forty-two years old and my father was fifty. They were barely holding it together, they could hardly put food on the table for us, and they were going to bring a new life into this world. I was silent, staring at the stained carpet below my feet. I think I began to count fleas. The house was completely infested with fleas. The only thing that protected me and my siblings from being devoured by these mean creatures was that my father could not afford to get flea treatment for our family dog, who suffered the brunt of these microscopic vampires.

"What were you thinking? And you are going to keep it?" I asked, as though it were any of my business.

I don't think that I was pro-choice. To be quite honest, I don't think that at fifteen I had a real understanding of what abortion was. Our church didn't even allow for dating, much less premarital sex, and so my reproductive understanding was admittedly very limited. I guess I figured they could take the child to a fire station or something. I was not interested in this child at all. I knew that it would mean more depression for my mother and less food to go around for us. It was an impractical decision and my parents were utterly irresponsible. I made that very clear to my parents. I can't imagine how deeply my cold response must have hurt my poor mother. For the remainder of her pregnancy, I was distant.

Be Our Guest

The homeless coalition was referencing more people over to our shelter than we could practically handle. Somehow, we made room one way or another for the majority of friends who called us looking for a place to stay. One day in the dead of winter, I received a call from a young grandmother who needed to find a place for herself, her daughter, and her granddaughter. They had been staying in a hotel for the last few weeks, using the grandmother's social security check. They reached the end and there was an even greater complexity that made their situation unique, she explained, "Now, she's pregnant."

"That isn't a problem. We have other women who have stayed here who are pregnant."

"Sir, I mean she could have that baby tonight."

And that is exactly what she did. Before we could even find a room for them at the shelter, the grandmother called me to let us know that her daughter's water had broken and they were off to the emergency room. All of the volunteer staff went into emergency mode trying to find a solution. We weren't exactly equipped to receive a newborn and mother in recovery. In reality, we weren't ready for a lot that fell on our plate that first winter, but we made it work somehow. We had a benefactor who committed a certain amount of funds for anything I considered a crisis. When he first offered that, I chuckled and said, "We are dealing with people being kicked out of their homes by slumlords or ending up on the streets because of house fires, everything is a crisis." I quickly learned that not all crises are created equal, and this was one of many moments where having that emergency fund was very beneficial. We made the decision that it was best to keep them in the hotel room they were in until we could figure out a better solution.

A few days later, I stopped by the hospital to meet the new mom and baby for the first time. They were unable to leave the hospital without presenting proof of a car seat. Sure, it was a practical rule, but what is a woman who is supporting her daughter and granddaughter—and now grandson!—supposed to do about a car seat when she's making all of this happen on $750 dollars a month plus food stamps?

I arrived with a brand new carseat that had been purchased by one of our volunteers and almost instantly found myself stuck in a whirlwind that felt very similar to the birth of my own children. Nurses were running in and out of the room and the mom asked if I would be willing to hold the baby while she got a few things ready. Within an hour we were out the door and I was strapping the brand new baby into my minivan and delivering them back to the hotel that was home for now.

As we pulled into the parking lot and made our way toward the back where their room was located, I couldn't stop the swell of emotions within me. In my lectures about the causes and effects of homelessness in America, there was a phrase I had often used to describe the moment when poverty transitions into the crisis of becoming legitimately unhoused. "The birth of homelessness," I would say with a dramatic pause. Well, here I was witnessing one of the most acute examples of that phrase. This child was literally being born into homelessness. What would his life become? Thirty years from now, would he come full circle and operate a homeless shelter in an attempt to save other women from his mother's fate, or would he be sucked into the prison pipeline?

Your Mother and Mine

I don't know if Mom went into labor during the day or night. Though I could tell you every single detail of the birth of my own children, those types of details of my own sibling's births are lost either to youth or just lack of concern for those sort of intricacies as a teenager. I do remember that I went to spend the night at my friend Paul's house. He was maybe the only person who really understood how dire our family's situation was. We had become quick friends as my parents attended a bible study at his house. Being close in age by only a few months meant that we experienced many of the same struggles and doubts concerning the faith of our parents.

If the birth of Aimee was anything like that of my other siblings, then I imagine I had spent a few days with my friend before the birth. I had spent the majority of that time playing video games with Paul and discussing how absolutely disinterested I was in my parents choice to bring another human being into this world. I don't think I was willing to admit even to my best friend that I had resolved in my own heart that I wouldn't even consider her like a real sibling. I had been through the war zone with my brother and sisters. This new addition was simply unwanted luggage. I still considered the most responsible thing for my parents to do would be to just drop her off at the nearest fire station, though I had not recommended that yet.

The phone rang.

"You are a big brother," my father declared, his voice choking slightly.

A thought began to form in my mind to protest that I was already a brother, and that this was not my sister. Then, a sense of duty and purpose welled up inside me. It propelled to the front of my thought process like a warrior with valor, sword drawn, slashing through the fog of my former disdain. The anger and bitterness melted away and my stone cold heart began to bleed red. Soon, I began to cry, though I concealed the emotion in my voice.

"I want to see her."

"We will come get you first thing in the morning."

"Now, Dad. I want to see my sister now."

Within half an hour my dad arrived. He instantly scolded me about how I was not to say anything that would upset my mother concerning the birth of the baby. Everyone was happy, he informed me. I did not have time to fight with my father about his perpetual distrust of me. I was a soldier on a mission, no sibling left behind.

We made it through the winding halls of the hospital and to the door with a large pink stork that read AIMEE. She had arrived—ready or not. I slowly opened the door and saw her small body wiggling around in the new world. I reached out my arms and cradled her, as I had done with the three others that preceded her. My father snapped a photo. I pulled her close to my face and whispered into her tiny ears, "Aimee, I am your big brother. I will never let anyone hurt you. I promise."

Soon, we would end up out of our not-home and back within the motel system. This time would be different and spawned by this new little life, my mother would finally be empowered to leave my father and my life would forever be changed. In many ways, I would fail at my promise to Aimee that day and our lives would go in very different directions. She would never know the life of poverty that the other siblings knew growing up, but my father's final attempt at holding onto my mother's love would force me away to make my own path. That decision would lead me to miss my youngest sister growing up, and in many ways my prophetic distance for those nine months came true. Though I kept my promise of protection by offering my mother what she truly needed, another promise altogether: that I would still love her if she left my father. It was in this falling apart, that everything finally came together.

5. Beauty and the Beast

"All right. I'm corny. But I think there's just about a-hundred-and-forty-million people in this country that are just as corny as I am." -Walt Disney

Someday My Prince Will Come

Nothing can distract us in youth like falling in love. All of the troubles of this world fade away in the excruciating saga of first kisses and the dramatic aching heart when we slowly extend a pinky finger, hoping that the person of our affections responds accordingly. However, these simple pleasures of life were strictly forbidden for the teenagers at the congregation our family attended.

Nashville is the closest thing there is to a Vatican City for Protestantism. We were the petri dish for every experimental ideology, whether in worship styles or sometimes even the advent of an entirely new theology. A growing contingent of baby boomers regretted their former lives of free love and drug abuse that they enjoyed as hippies. Now, they had been saved by the Jesus Movement that tailed in on the end of the 70's. They started to have families and mortgages and needed to be baptized out of their youthful ambitions to find a purpose, and ideally a decent salary with dental. Many co-opted the dress and musical style of their generation and transitioned it into one of the fastest growing movements within Christianity since the first apostles showed up on the scene with free food and medical.

It was the CCM (Contemporary Christian Movement) crowd that propelled my father to a certain level of fame in the 70's and early 80's. He traveled the globe and even flew his own plane as Donny Monk and Friends took on the world with music that sounded like the spirit of the age, but drew people into the semi-traditional model of mainstream Christianity. It was just like remaining a hippy, except militantly anti-gay. Many of these young artists like Leon Patilio, Dave Williamson, Michael W. Smith, and Steven Curtis Chapman all migrated to Nashville as if it were the Mecca of the new wave of free musical expression within the Christian context. Not since Martin Luther melded bar music with the Psalms had worship music resounded so effectively.

In spite of his own contribution to the CCM experiment, my dad missed the original boat ride to Nash Vegas and by the time he finally did move us to Music City, the older generation was already in the process of handing over the reins to their younger, more tech savvy offspring. They had already built a name and a legacy to pass on, having made their own record labels and recording studios. Dad came back on the scene half a decade too late to revive his career. His music was already antiquated and everything was already flashier and faster. The world had moved on without him and it would be to their loss, I might add.

The older frontrunners of the Christian recording industry started to become pastors and authors, traveling the world peddling their new ideas on the faith. Much of their ideology rebuked the supposed mistakes of their generation and tried to prevent all of us young folks from making the same choices. Losing sight, of course, of the importance that choice plays in all aspects of life, religion not excluded. They plowed forward with an ambition to save souls, and subsequently, the virginity of all who would listen.

I grew up immersed in the sudden explosion of the True Love Waits phenomenon. A young homeschooled kid like myself had written a book condemning the entire practice of dating. Though I highly doubt that the idea was his own, it was still packaged as the mused youthful pondering of an enlightened spiritual leader who could speak to all the less enlightened young perverts who might want to see someone naked. He philosophized this: essentially, dating leads to hand holding, and that leads to kissing, and then groping, and after that baby making. The easiest way to avoid the sin of carnal pleasure was to never put yourself into the initial situation to begin with.

The pastor of our church had a relatively attractive teenage daughter and he desperately wanted to preserve her chastity, and so logically the anti-dating mentality soon became dogma. If there was no dating, then no young men could come around to woo her. It was perfect logic, minus the fact that it was fighting hormones and the irrational mind of humans without a fully developed frontal lobe. I had many a friend who lost their virginity fully clothed or through holes in sheets because where there is a will, there is a completely screwed up way to create a loophole around fundamentalism.

It is no wonder then, that boys and girls quickly found themselves creating best friends with whomever they were attracted to. No adult could bat an eyelash at these young people on fire for God, so chaste that they were able to maintain these truly pure relationships. However, soon these little prayer pow wows gave way to temporal pleasures. There is a reason that the original humans wanted to eat the only fruit they weren't allowed to have. Tell kids that they can have every candy on the aisle except for the one in the purple wrapper and you will have children eating themselves sick on only that style, leaving the entire rest of the stash untouched. Prohibiting sex is just like that, except with teen pregnancy instead of cavities.

Like many of my peers, I had formed a best friend type of relationship with a young woman and we were highly committed to our juvenile love. When we turned eighteen we would be wed, like many of the seniors ahead of us. Then our affections would be solidified with a first kiss at the altar in the church and our forever love would seal our fate, soon leading to children. Trivial things like work and education were of little significance when Jesus would return within our own lifetime. All that mattered was the preservation of our virginity and our undeniable purity for the Lord.

SOMETHING THERE

I think that it is nearly impossible to tell the story of how you fall in love. What feels like love in the beginning, and what it becomes, are two very distinct and separate things. In a way, it almost feels like there are two different people: the person I met and the person I married. Now, I realize that sounds like a negative, but it really isn't. When we meet someone, we come into it with a certain level of prejudice and judgment. We assume a great deal about this person and that, of course, plays into the attraction. It is that mystery of wanting to discover if we are right or wrong that keeps passion alive. Is this person beautiful naked? Are their stories interesting? Do they want children? This is, in essence, the art of dating. Discovering another person's body, mind, and soul, and finding if their pieces fit the missing pieces in you. Although it is arguably healthier if the whole pieces of you compliment the whole parts of them. And visa versa. But, of course, humans rarely do what is healthiest for them. We are fundamentally flawed in that way.

However, I never dated my future wife. Our first date was the night that I proposed and it would quickly become the last date we would attend together for some time, because we weren't simply getting married, we were starting a family. Ready or not, here it comes.

Tashina attacked my life like a violent hurricane rushing and conquering on the stem of a delicate flower. She was beautiful and wrathful, intelligent and utterly impractical, bombarding and yet deeply wounded. She loved me from the moment she saw me and I ran like hell.

Ours was not a classic love story and, by most standards, it was exasperatingly complicated. When we met, she had just recently had a baby and was also engaged, but not in love, with the child's father. I had just recently been ordained and was considering a vow of celibacy, at which I was dramatically failing.

I think that one of the most fascinating parts about being in a relationship, especially a long term one, is that you are able to see life from other angles. People pass you on the streets or read about you on social media and build opinions of who you are. This happens countless times in a day and rarely will you ever know what that person thinks of you. Maybe if they choose to start a rumor about you then you could certainly hear about it, but the reality is that for most of us, the passing feelings or judgments of society will remain a mystery to us for the majority of our lives. However, a relationship opens the door to all of the different judgments and scandals and missing pieces that add up to the whole that is known as life.

Had Tashina and I never met and fallen in love, I would have never known all of the amazing pieces of the puzzle that brought us together, and it can be that quick, too. A missed connection. One wrong number and the telephone call never comes. The child who would grow up to be the doctor who cures cancer … his entire life depends on restaurant parking.

As life would have it, while I was living my life and the drama of it was unfolding before the very eyes of the world, some were fascinated, others were infuriated, and somewhere else, a young man was throwing a newspaper in front of his soon-to-be bride, quipping that the man on the front page might be a more suitable life mate for her than he was. I often wonder if he knew in that moment that he was literally introducing his fiancé to the man she would one day marry. If he would have not wasted the quarter or purchased a magazine instead. But as life is, we rarely have the ability to see how certain mundane actions can have long-term butterfly effects on our destiny.

So, Tashina picked up that paper and read the title, "First Amendment Crusader." She determined that I might very well be the person she was looking for—if not in a life partner, certainly as a friend. But how would she find me? The paper always had a convenient way of ignoring the fact that I really did have a church and a location where it met. But that need to find me would be absolutely irrelevant, because as it turns out, I would find her.

One night after a long day hanging out with my best friend, we decided to step into a Waffle House for some late night reenergizing. On my stroll to our regular booth, there sat a large Irish man by the name of Murphy. He and I were drinking buddies from McGuire's, the local Irish pub. Murphy received great amusement out of drinking with a priest and I got equal amusement out of hanging out with a bear-man who cussed like a sailor and cried like a baby every time Danny Boy played on the bagpipes.

There he sat, taking up one side of the booth for his girth, and the other was allotted to two young women. Now, if you had asked Murphy, he would have told you that it would take two women to settle him, and whereas there was no argument that he was enough mass for two men, the reality is that women adored him as one of the sweetest and gentlest men they had met. He was the constant protector and big brother. In all of his talk of womanizing, the reality is that he truly loved and adored women. He is a charming fellow.

There he sat, laughing from his belly and entertaining as usual. Nothing was particularly different about the night, other than that one of the women sitting there at the table was the future mother of my children. But I certainly had no future knowledge of that. Had I possessed the gentlemanliness to have looked her in the eyes, I would have instantly seen it. Staring back at me from those deep brown orbs would have been a dark sadness melting away as she looked at me. I would have seen visions of travel, houses, heartache, and unending love. But as it was, I saw none of those things. I simply quickly glanced at a beautiful body in a sleek dress and immediately decided I would make an impression at poor Murphy's expense. I quickly noticed the element of my humor. Adorning the neck of the Irish brute was a long celtic rosary with a gigantic crucifix and corpus lying across his stomach. Without a moment of hesitation, I walked directly up to the table.

"You've got my boss around your neck, I see," I said.

"We all work for him in our way."

"Sure, but I think he owes me a dental package."

And with that, I picked up the corpus and put it to my ear, as if the rosary was a telephone, and began to have a long one-sided conversation with the Lord of the Universe via Murphy's necklace, discussing the need for a better severance package and medical insurance. I continued on amusing my audience and then at some sly moment introduced myself to the young women with the man. We chatted for a while and with that—entertaining accomplished and affection dually received—I left without a second thought.

If life were such that I could relive moments, I am certain I would go back to that one and listen to hear stories and hurts and fresh wounds. But that may very well be the worst thing I could do. Because in that moment, unbeknownst to me, I had poured water all over the recently planted seed in her heart. So maybe it is best that currently feminist me should butt out of my formerly misogynistic tendencies and let love take its burning and life-altering course. It is this lover that would change the course of my heart and mind forever.

Later, we would meet again at a local pool hall on her birthday. She told me that she always hated birthdays because they never ended well. So I decided to serenade her from atop a barstool and lead the entire room in a rendition of happy birthday. What I didn't know then—like a great many other things I clearly didn't know—is that this would begin a long tradition of making good birthdays. We parted ways, but before I did I invited her to come over one Sunday night. She obliged, but she almost didn't make it through the front door. Hell, she almost didn't get out of her car. But again, it seemed the universe was rooting for us.

We were still meeting on Sunday nights at my parent's house in "the basement" and without question our church was mostly a boy's club. It was a rag tag team of social misfits that probably couldn't have gotten girlfriends if they wanted to, but fortunately most of them didn't want to. The few girls that did attend were their honorary besties who had long ago "friend zoned" them. Though I have grown to deplore the term, it was none-the-less the running gag of the group. Tashina arrived with her sister and when she saw our group of men all dressed in black band t-shirts and smoking cigarettes, she began to have second thoughts. Actually, she had a lot of thoughts on the subject that she later verbalized to her sister before they exited the car.

"What if this is some trick to lure young women to their cult? What if these guys are dangerous? What if they are going to kill us?"

Clearly, she had emotional issues. But for whatever reasons, despite these fears, she decided to give it one chance. And one chance only. She stepped out of the car, ready to face whatever reaction it would be, all of these fears and anxieties on the forefronts of their minds. One of the young men looked directly at Tashina as she exited the vehicle, and as if to answer the questions that were pressing in her psyche, he simply uttered, "No. It won't happen."

In her own mind, she determined this was fate letting her know that none of those fears were valid and she stepped right into my life. We later questioned our friend about the motivation behind his random "no," but he offered no real answers. He was always a quirky individual. But I have to remain eternally grateful for his weirdness that night.

After the service ended and everyone left, we spent the entire evening under the stars. She sat on the hood of her car smoking through a pack of cigarettes and I paced back and forth as we debated life and love, philosophy and religion. We could not have been more opposite. As cutting edge as I may have appeared to this town, at my core, I was relatively fundamentalist at heart. She was bold and daring and unashamed. I was ashamed and guilt-stricken about every aspect of my life—about my sexual desires, my hopes for the future, and fear was an underlying theme that ran like a rushing current through my mind. Even her experience with homelessness as a youth runaway acted as a contrast to my own, which was thrust upon me by exterior circumstances. Now, the more I know, I can see so clearly that her running away was not a rebellion. It was survival. For these, and so many other reasons, it was clear that she was quite literally the closest thing I had ever met to a truly free spirit.

But that freedom came with a price.

In that conversation, I learned that she had a child who was not yet one and that she was engaged. She identified as being both pagan and queer. She spoke freely about her mother's murder and how deeply it had affected her. The candor with which she shared these stories, with no sense of irony, was so foreign to me.

After our talk, I allowed that fear to grip me by the throat and drag me into the worst parts of myself, the hell that lived inside my own soul. It was full of self-loathing, misogyny, and worst of all, a religious spirit that I was attempting to combat outwardly, but was still allowing to dictate my inward actions. As attracted as I was to her, how could I possibly date a pagan, bisexual, single mother? Didn't this combat every thing that I, as a priest, was supposed to stand for? And so here I stood on the precipice of my first battle for marriage equality and I didn't even know it. I couldn't even see it. Mostly because I could barely grapple within myself that I was now being seen as some soldier on the forefront of civil rights. How could I possibly see myself, the son of a southern Baptist minister turned priest, as someone who would soon be fighting for the right for love to transcend gender, sexuality, and any other differences we create in our society?

Every minute that I could fashion an excuse, I would spend with her. She returned the ring she had received and told the man she was to marry that she had, in fact, fallen for the boy from the papers. A month later, we would share a passionate kiss by the moonlight and crashing waves after a heated debate about the legitimacy of the Bush presidency.

But I would fail at loving her. I would push her away and back into the arms of the man she rejected for our love. She would marry him and I would decide I loved another. And the story would seem nearly finished until a little tiny hand reached into mine. And with those same brown eyes as her mother, looked up at mine, and said, "Daddy."

HELLFIRE

The young and innocent love of the hyper-fundamentalist youth can be very confusing. How much we believed the dramatic warnings that were imposed on us by our church as teens was debatable. We feared our parents far more than the wrath of God. Mothers at the church were taught to make occasional accusations of wrongdoing in hopes to catch their children in lies. It made the mothers seem prophetic, as if the Eye of God followed us around and reported back like a playground tattletale. I began to really resent God for this. He gave us freewill and then reported back to our moms like it was the Hoover administration.

My father was doing some part-time work for the church to work off a debt to them he had acquired when they offered financial assistance to pay overdue bills. He had been tasked with a clerical position doing some type editing.

There had recently been a schism in the congregation by which the minister of music had left rather dramatically. About half of those who attended the church left as a result of this and it was time for the pastor to clean up shop. My family stayed behind, despite my father's friendship with the music minister, but the pastor of our church was about to push the limits of my father's abilities to remain silent.

The split was causing a crisis for those of us in the youth program. Friends were dropping left and right, being pulled away by their parents, caught up in the politics of religion. My now secret fiancé's parents were part of the pastor's inner circle. Little did I know, my father was placing himself in a position to go all Capulet without warning. My seemingly mild mannered father was going to grow a pair at one of the most inconvenient times of my adolescence.

The pastor announced that he wished for the websites and brochures to be updated, excluding any reference to the minister of music who helped found the church. The now mini-mega church had been formed in the minister of music's home, along with ten other families, and grew quickly from there. However, that narrative seemed utterly inconvenient to the pastoral dictatorship that was left behind. His demands of the revisionist history did not sit well with my father, who argued that even the New Testament authors chose to keep the stories of their disagreements in our holy texts. It was a flawless argument, but logic and reason are rarely appreciated by power hungry men who are building an empire of teenage virgins ready for the apocalypse.

Soon, everything came crashing down. My love and I were torn apart by our now feuding families. But another issue arose without the safety net of our congregation. Our family reached another peak of instability which led us directly back off the cliff of poverty and into the valley of the shadow of death.

6. TIMON AND PUMBAA

"I'm always thinking of what's wrong with the thing and how it can be improved."

- Walt Disney

A FRIEND LIKE ME

The day I turned seventeen was when everything changed. The year leading up to this moment had brought about many unique opportunities. After leaving our church, I found a new group of friends, was working a part time job at a store in the mall, and took up acting. My social schedule gave me a reprieve from the insanity of the world I lived in. I had recently been cast in a made-for-TV movie that wrapped over the previous summer. My life was a series of bizarre juxtapositions. During the day I would be on random film sets for music videos, commercials, or movies. I would leave our impoverished life to ride in limousines with fellow rising actors.

One of the most predominant make-up and special effects artists in Nashville had taken me under his wing. After years of working in salons, Jasper had learned how to be a stylist/therapist to the stars. He had traveled around the world working with celebrities of every variety. Soon, I was working with him on my off days, grabbing brushes and other supplies like a surgeons assistant. He was one of the first adults I could really talk to about my parents. I soon realized that not all adults were on the same team. By the time I started my part-time job at the mall, my ability to trust had really flourished. Johnny, my boss, also took me in, becoming a father figure to me as well. He was my immediate supervisor and he considered it his personal mission to make sure that he instilled in me a work ethic and an appropriate level of snark.

After spending many years of estrangement with my own father, I suddenly found myself with two dads willing to invest in me and teach me their trade. This also stretched the limits of the fundamentalism I had grown up in, because both of these men were gay.

I do not remember anyone ever directly sitting me down one day and telling me that being gay was a sin. It was not something that was discussed often, at least not in our home. But like many things, the idea found its way in the subtle teachings. The more I got involved within the acting community, the more I began to make friends with people, both young and old, who identified with many different variables of the LGBTQ community. I was beginning to see a major disconnect between what I was being taught in Sunday School and the reality I experienced in my own life.

After leaving the church that we were a part of, I reverted back to our Baptist roots. I needed a break from the circus of the charismatic fundamentalism I had been inundated with for the majority of my teenage years. I started attending a mega church within the Southern Baptist flavor. For all of their own fundamentalist undercurrents, they were lacking in many of the elements that I was attempting to flee from. There were no teachings condemning dating and the End of Days was set well in the future, not some imminent event we all needed to either fear or prepare for. No longer having to deal with the anxieties of a sword wielding Jesus returning to consume the world in judgment and fire, released me to love God again. For a while, I had grown to see God in the same way I saw my own father, a man who had abandoned me emotionally and only came around to cast disparagement and punishment. I was far too self-unaware to realize that my narrow and incorrect view of both God and my father came from the same source. It seems that deities and parents are far too complex to put into such small boxes.

One Sunday morning, I attended class with the rest of my grade. When I arrived, I found listed on the dry erase board a litany of sins, prohibitions, and generally damnable offenses. The teacher was fixated on only one though: being queer. So he preached and ranted to the forty or fifty of us sitting in our cushioned metal chairs. One kid over to my right looked uneasy, and a sadness hung over him like a large rain cloud with a rainbow shining through the top, flashing so the whole world could see how gay he was. His countenance screamed that he would rather be dead than be sitting there in that class, and in that moment, I bet that was true.

I raised my hand.

"Yes, the newcomer in the back."

"Do you masturbate?" I asked, not really skipping a beat.

"Excuse me?"

"I mean, like, do you jerk off?"

"That is inappropriate. We are not going to discuss that here."

"Well, I mean we are discussing two guys doing it. I don't see how you doing it alone is somehow more inappropriate of a subject matter than that, and when my mom asked me that question and I didn't answer, she took that as a yes."

"Is there a point?"

"Yeah, there is a point. I mean, there is a whole list of sins there, not just being gay. Adultery is right there too, right? So if you masturbate, and you think about a girl other than your wife, I mean, you are right up there with the gay guy, right? You are no different. So why are we sitting here, judging, when you are an adulterating masturbator?" I was quite the master debater... of theology, you pervert.

I was told I could hold any more questions until after class and so I did. I actually didn't have any other questions and once the class was dismissed, the guy didn't really make an effort to come correct me or anything. I am sure he had determined my naughty soul was already damned. Wouldn't be the first or last time I would be written off as a lost cause in the religious realm. When I walked out, there was the kid waiting for me. He asked me if we could talk and so we went to the mall. His name was Jeff. He told me he was gay and I told him that was cool, and that I cared about him anyway, and so did Jesus.

See, the thing is, in that moment I loved him despite the fact that he was gay. Sure, I cared about him, I didn't judge him—at least not in a certain sense, not like that Sunday school teacher did—but I still hoped that one day Jeff would be fixed or something. I also thought that the Sunday School teacher should stop beating it too.

The two worlds I was living in to relieve the pain of our poverty and homelessness were in direct conflict with each other. It was a dichotomy that I would not fully address until much later in life. For while toting the party line on marriage equality, I would be revolutionary amongst my peers in the priesthood. I would advocate for gay adoption because of my experience with the two men who had become dads to me when I needed one so desperately. I would support the idea of civil unions, but I would fall short in many ways. My fundamentalism would hold onto a portion of my heart throughout the years until it finally reached a point of no return and I was forced to make a decision.

LOVE IS AN OPEN DOOR

The Facebook post tab stared back at me as if it were the red button a president pushes to launch a nuclear weapon. I lingered back at it, realizing that in my own little way I had the same burden as a head of state about to send a warhead out into the universe. The decision I was about to make would have ripple effects I would never be able to see. Some would view my words as salvation, and others would believe that they damned my soul.

For years, I sat on the fence concerning the issue of marriage equality. It was irresponsible of me, but I also knew that the price was very high. When I first entered the church, the issues of homosexuality and the Bible were minor issues. Now, I say that from the vantage point of being a straight white cis male. Undoubtedly, the church's stance on the LGBTQ community has had major effects on the lives of queer people. When I say it was a minor issue, I mean that it was not the hottest theological discussion point amongst Catholic and Orthodox clerics. We knew what we were supposed to say if the issue arose and most of us ignored it.

Most Orthodox priests I knew had gay couples and families that attended their congregations, many of which served on parish councils or boards.

As long as everyone kindly ignored the issue of marriage, everything was fine. Sure, the occasional priest would go all "canon law" on someone by refusing communion and everyone would instantly have to do the moderate shuffle. We would publicly affirm our commitment to the canons of the church, marriage is between one man and one woman, and then pick up the phone and call all our LGBTQ parishioners to make use they understood they were still welcome. The whole thing followed the military's code of "don't ask, don't tell." For a while, this seemed to be a normalized balance. But then people started asking and telling all over the place. Marriage equality was reaching a boiling point in our nation and everyone was picking sides. This whole thing would be a lot easier if the bishops would admit they were gay, stop oppressing the masses, and we could move on in peace, but as one of my spiritual fathers often said, "The Orthodox Church would be perfect if it weren't for all these goddamn people."

I got closer to the fire than most of my peers. Our congregation even counter-protested the openly bigoted bible thumpers who would show up in the styles of Westboro Baptist Church and picket the events surrounding gay pride week in Pensacola. Myself and my parishioners would arrive with signs of love and tolerance.

But that word—tolerance—covers a great many sins, doesn't it? I mean, we were taught to tolerate murderers, adulterers, and any other prohibitions in the scripture. If someone was willing to repent, or at least seem to show some form of reform (or just keep their opinions and feelings to themselves), then compassion was given. The problem with applying this idea of toleration to LGBTQ individuals is that you choose to murder someone or commit adultery. Those are actions someone does, not something they are. To say that we tolerated gay people was to say there was something intrinsically wrong with them and we were just getting over that. I don't tolerate someone's race or gender. I accept those things about them. Better yet, I don't have a choice but to accept those things because that is just who they are.

The Church was becoming more polarized and each person took their side of the corner in the boxing ring. I was simply trying to play referee. And then something shifted.

Each year, the number of homeless youth was growing exponentially and the majority of them were ending up on the streets because of their sexual identity. Families were literally throwing their children out on the streets or forcing them to run away because of who their children were. This wasn't happening because parents have a natural fear of children liking someone of the same sex or because they are trans, this was happening as a hyper reaction to the dramatic stances many in the hierarchy were making on the issue. What was once a back burner issue was now becoming the dividing line of who was a true Christian or not. It became apparent that the church believed that to love Jesus meant you had to reject people who were gay.

Teens were ending up homeless or committing suicide because religion was painting them as villains for something they couldn't change about themselves. The time to sit on the fence had come to an end. Tashina and I tried desperately to put together a "practical" exit strategy. After all, this had been our entire life together. My daughters had only known life within the church and we had a son on the way. We needed to be responsible. We wouldn't be given that opportunity, however.

While still living in South Carolina, we visited a plantation outside of Charleston. During a portion of the self-guided tour we walked down a small village of slave cabins. As we stepped into one of them, the set up inside was noticeably different than the others. It was the chapel. Inside, there was a replica of a hand-written sermon by a pastor explaining to the slaves why God condoned their slavery. It was rampant with scriptures and biblical analogy. I stopped to read it with tears forming in my eyes.

I suppose like most people, I believed that if I had lived during the Holocaust I would have hidden Jews. Or if I lived during the Civil Rights Movement, I would have marched with Dr. King. But here I was standing silent as millions of people across my own country and across the globe were being denied fundamental rights due to be fact that they were gay. I was part of a church that not only actively supported this oppression, but in many cases the bishops were participants in writing similar sermons, all using scripture, all supported theologically, but lacking in the spirit of an almighty and loving God. Just as verses could be found to support slavery, and yet those verses are now rejected, I became certain in that moment that this prohibition upon marriage for all people would be rejected too. I had been silent too long and if I was not careful, it could be one of my own sermons sitting immortalized as a symbol of this wicked era that prohibited love.

The power of equality was moving like a wildfire and on the day the Supreme Court made the decision to strike down DOMA, my fellow clergymen decided to show the ugliest side of religious piety. Hundreds of posts began to flood all levels of social media condemning those who identified as LGBTQ.

Many people claimed that this would be the end of society as we knew it. Others prayed that AIDs would swiftly wipe out all of them before the real virus of homosexuality infected the world. As if this wasn't shocking enough, some even encouraged gay youth to take their own lives. I couldn't help but wonder where the Jesus—who loved indiscriminately—stood in all of this.

So I wrote a letter resigning from active ministry in the Church and pushed that button and launched WWIII.

Within minutes I was flooded with death threats and condemnations. One monk even called me on my cell phone to scream in my ear that I was a heretic and that I would burn in hell. The church sent a high ranking official to my house in less than a day to present me with letters of excommunication and I was officially defrocked.

Priests who have molested children receive less harsh sentences.

Within a few days, my family went into hiding and left like refugees in the middle of the night. After we finished packing the car and I sat down behind the driver's seat, the realizations hit me that we really failed at having a plan. There was no back up career. We had no destination. And I was suddenly gripped with fear. Would we end up homeless? Was I about to repeat the sins of my father?

A VERY MERRY UNBIRTHDAY

After the end of my seventeenth birthday party, my mother packed my sisters in the car and left for Pensacola, Florida. My siblings and I had spent many a summer there with my grandmother. My grandparents decided to retire there after my grandpa ended his military career. Mom was finally breaking free of Nashville and making the decision to move on. If my father decided to follow, he could only do so if things were finally stable. My younger brother moved into a motel with my dad near the hobby store he was working part-time, and I moved into Johnny's apartment.

For those brief months living with him, my life finally had a sense of calm and peace. I worked at a bakery and took acting gigs on the side. I had friends and stability. He would take me on road trips to art exhibits. Though Johnny and Jasper both knew each other—because let's face it, the gay community in the highly religious community of

Nashville was relatively small—they were not what you would call friends. It felt a bit like having divorced gay dads, bouncing back and forth in a shared custody.

One day, there was a knock at the door. It was my biological father. He and Johnny spoke briefly and coldly, and then Dad entered our home. He was going to visit my mother in Pensacola and wanted to know if I would go with him. I desperately wanted to see my mother and sisters. I quickly packed my bags and gave Johnny a hug and told him I loved him. It would only be a few days.

It was a relaxing trip and it was good to see my sisters, though Aimee barely remembered me. Finally, the day arrived for my return back to Nashville. Though I loved my sisters, I was building a new life. I had my own job and money. Soon Johnny was going to finally teach me how to drive. Dad told me he would pick me up at my grandmother's house in the morning, but he was late. My father is never late. I called his cell phone, but it went to voicemail. I tried again and he answered.

"Dad, where are you?"

"I am on my way back to Nashville."

"You are supposed to pick me up! I have to be at work tomorrow."

"You are my son and it is time for me to bring our family back together under one roof. I will gather your things from Johnny's. You need to be with your family."

I wanted to say something hurtful. I wanted to denounce him as my father and hitchhike my way back to Nashville, but I was only seventeen years old. Though I felt like I had been kidnapped, the reality was that if I left that bitter afternoon, I would be viewed as a runaway. I was trapped. All I wanted to do was to get out of this one stoplight redneck town. I swore in that moment that this wouldn't be the end. I was not going to live my life in some washed up place like Pensacola.

7. Fidelity Fiduciary Bank

"You may not realize it when it happens, but a kick in the teeth may be the best thing in the world for you."
- Walt Disney

Someday

I was quickly becoming distracted by life in the small town that was not becoming home, but a menial prison. Soon, I was dating, making friends, and found there was a thriving theatre community that took me in. It kept me busy and kept my mind off of the fact that I was stuck in a town that was light-years behind what I was used to after living in one of the major entertainment centers in America. What Pensacola lacked in a social scene, it made up for in pure southern charm with a side of Waffle House sweet tea.

The sadness and disdain for my own life was growing a dark garden deep in my heart. There was so much unresolved conflict. Our home life felt like a charade of Cleaverdom. Dad finally found a full-time job and we had a home that wasn't a squatter. The van was parked nicely in our driveway. Our family heirlooms were in the garage and not a pay-by-the-month storage unit constantly in fear of being sold off to the highest bidder. In many ways things were stabilizing, but much like a soldier who comes home unable to truly leave the war, I was stricken with PTSD as I waited for any sound to flash me back to the traumas of combat. Any time it seemed that the electricity might not be paid, a tightness would seize my chest. I feared we would spend another night hoping the food didn't spoil. I would hear a loud knock at the door and wonder if the police were arriving to tell us our time was up at the motel.

We were living in a house in my grandmother's neighborhood that had been the home of one of my mother's friends growing up. His family had founded the local rescue mission for the homeless. My grandfather and mother used to volunteer there when she was a teenager. My grandpa helped install the heating and cooling units there. My mother sorted clothing in their thrift stores. That family held onto the their old family home and now my father was renting it. For my mother, life had come full circle in many ways. Just as I had longed so desperately to make it back to the safety of the town that I called home, she was finally back in a place that brought her a sense of peace and stability. She knew that if my father relapsed into his poverty addiction, that she could walk down the street to the security of her own fond childhood memories nestled in the cedar-planked closets of my grandmother's home.

I graduated high school that year. No cap and gown. No superintendent commencing me to my next destination in life. No grand speeches warning about drugs, alcohol, and ambition. I was not advised to shoot for the stars, but to settle for normalcy. No, this is how my graduation ceremony was conducted:

I arrived at the house one night and my mother pointed at a pile of mail on the kitchen table. A large envelope set at the top with my name written across it. I delicately opened the package and pulled out my diploma. In the time since my original diagnosis with dyslexia, I had gone from being a child with little hope of ever reading or writing to a young man graduating a year early. This diploma acted in my mind as a stepping-stone toward my ultimate prison break. Our time of poverty had made me feral and this new found "home" was feeling more like captivity. I felt as if my parents hadn't earned the right to domesticate me, I was my own person now, and it was time to set me free. If they weren't going to do it willingly, I would make my escape. And I knew exactly how I would do it.

Before my grandfather died, he had set up military credit union accounts for the grandchildren he had met. My grandmother kept the tradition and placed small funds in them on our birthday, slowly they would accrue a modest interest. We would receive these accounts on our eighteenth birthday and mine was quickly approaching. I knew I would be able to use it to enroll in college, go on a self-discovery trip, or as I was beginning to fantasize, I would be able to escape back home to Nashville and restart my life were it had left off. Nothing could hold me back. A new life awaited me and I could smell freedom in the air.

RIFF RAFF, STREET RAT

Our food sharing program was continuing to grow each week, and hundreds of homeless and poor people lined up to receive a hot meal on Thursday nights, their feet shuffling in the dust as they lined the sidewalk under the I-110 overpass.

This was not our ideal location. It was a compromise with the city fathers who no longer wanted us to meet in one of the beautiful parks downtown. This project began with humble enough beginnings; volunteers bringing side dishes and my father bringing southern fried chicken and biscuits. He would sing a few songs and I would give my best shot at an inspirational message. In tandem, as the number of those in need of food would grow, so would the interest by folks within the community to volunteer their time.

What was initially a small gathering of older homeless men who slept on benches under shady trees, quickly drew out people from the surrounding slums just outside of the main strip of retail stores and bars along Palafox Street. The downtown area was finally building a small audience and a great deal of effort had gone into trying to reduce crime and blight, but that term "blight" can be used to cover a great many visual discomforts to investors: a diseased tree, a dilapidated building, and, of course, poor people. Our little meetings with the impoverished in the park garnered attention to the forgotten lepers in town, still hiding in the darker outskirts just a few streets away from the now prime real estate.

First, we started to notice police cars surrounding the perimeters of the park. Soon, an officer or two would sit outside of their cars and watch our activities. Finally, one day we were approached by an officer who gave me a directive to make contact with the City Administrators office. I made an appointment and sat alone at a table full of men in suits and ties. I was given the ultimatum of either being shut down or to move quite literally to the wrong side of the tracks. As in, directly next to the train tracks, adjacent to the housing projects, wedged next a homeless shelter, you know, "Where people are more accustomed to this sort of thing." Had I been more savvy, as I later would become, I likely would have put up a fight. But this was my first engagement with local politics and these guys play a mean game of intimidation, especially for a twenty-year-old boy mildly uncertain as to why he had freely returned to this godforsaken place after finally escaping. Hadn't I, in no uncertain terms, said, "Anywhere but Pensacola?"

Unaware of how much weight a decent attorney and a good ole fashioned sit in could wield, I took the compromise at face value. So there we were under the noisy overpass, no longer shaded by beautiful trees, but by hard cement and florescent lights that flickered in protest of their disrepair. As if the poor needed another reminder as to where the City thought they fit in society, this move acted as a perfect punctuation to their not-so-subtle explanation. As it was explained to us, there was a grave concern about what effect so much foot traffic might have on the grass, and grass, as you know, is expensive. Slowly, I would begin to notice that there seemed to be less of a concern when the grass was crushed by middle class white feet during special events. Hell, that was highly encouraged! I would also soon notice that not only were these people encouraged to bring their trampling feet downtown, but they could also eat in the park or even drink beer and wine. Which was an offense our homeless friends would have been quickly arrested for. There was a great disparity in how those with and those without are treated. I would later re-engage the debate over that park's use, but for the time being, I was more concerned about making sure that those in my care were fed and warm. If these city officials were so willing to brush these folks under the rug, I would not simply be a food distribution point, but also a friend. In my own experience of homelessness, it had been the value of friendship that invested itself into my life and helped me rise above. It was once people stopped seeing my parents' need, and just started seeing me, that a true change took place.

There was a middle-aged woman who I loved to see each week. She was colorful and flamboyant.

We became quick friends, laughing and sharing stories. Each week, she waited toward the front of the line and would always ask me if I could give her estimations as to what each meal would cost in the stores. I would rattle off numbers based upon what we paid for the portions that we had out-of-pocket expenses for, and give my best guess at what a six pound tub of green beans would cost, divided by a hundred and twenty hungry souls. She would take out a small black journal from her purse and make minor notations.

"Let me have a breast, preacher. I just love those breasts!"

Everyone wanted a breast. I tried desperately to be fair in how we distributed the chicken, but everyone knew that those at the end of the line had less of a chance. How could I refuse her robust personality? It was moments like this that made it all worth it. The smiles. The flashing moments of joy. "One day, Chicken Man, those sons of bitches will pay, and when they do… you'll get yours back. Everyone who ever helped me will." And with that, she would close her book, place it delicately back in its proper place in her bag, and take her plate to find her place amongst the dust. There were no masterfully antiquated benches to sit on in the ghetto.

Each week was exactly the same with her and the more she came through, the more her story took shape in my mind. Apparently, according to her, she had been hurt on the job and that was what led to her unemployment, and eventually her homelessness.

"I'm not lazy, preacher. No, sir! I worked too goddamn hard. Excuse my words. Praise Jesus! But just too goddamn hard, and Lord Jesus knows I didn't know those sons of bitches wouldn't pay when I hurt myself. They gonna be paying now! Praise the Lord, you just wait."

However, after my recent brushes with the government, I was not so certain that she would be that lucky. Not to mention, just like prison and church, everyone has an amazing testimony out here. I was becoming jaded trying to figure who really invented the "spaceship needs parts" panhandling sign, and also which folks really did arrive on spaceships. I chalked this woman's story up to hopeful ambition—escapism to make this horrible reality less painful, and God knows I had used similar techniques to survive my own time on the streets and motels of America.

Many years later, a large black Cadillac SUV with spinning wheels pulled up next to me, and a large woman would burst through its doors. Her hair flowed in a million colorful directions and her long nails bewildered me. How could she properly navigate that beast of a vehicle with those nails?

She accosted me with a hug, rocking my entire frame back and forth in giant thrusts of joy as she screamed, "Praise Jesus!"

Finally, she released her powerful grip, took me by the shoulders, and looked me square in the eyes. Then I realized that her face looked familiar and under all of the new hair and make-up, I saw my friend.

"Chicken Man! Those bitches paid. They paid me every penny."

And with that, she opened a small black journal, looking for the proper inscription. She smiled and opened up an envelope and pulled out an exact amount of cash.

"I've paid everyone back. You all helped me and now I'm just paying it back. I told you I would!"

Then, just as quickly as she came rushing back into my life, she disappeared. We purchased a little extra fried chicken that night and everyone got chicken breasts in her honor.

Later, I took on the issue of the park again and fought for the right to distribute food to those in need. I wanted to make sure that the parks were not segregated amongst the "haves" and the "have nots". It wouldn't be long until I'd discover a fight against social injustice that would lead to another spoke on a wheel I would have never known was connected, but yet here it was, churning the mill of oppression. Because of these infamous poverty-related fights with the city, one day I was invited to visit a top attorney in the nation. We met in his office, lined with artifacts my inner Indiana Jones would argue should be more fitting in museums. After our conversation moved from casual talk to business, we made our way down a long hallway, past numerous employees propelling the machine of this man's legend, and finally, to our destination. The board room where our lunch would arrive.

As we waited for our food, he recounted stories of his own childhood poverty. Before he was a multimillionaire, he had lived in cars and bounced around amongst relatives. It was his own struggle that motivated him to fight against injustice and take on major corporations. His way of helping to solve the problem of poverty was to fight on behalf of those who were seen as small. They were David, the corporations were Goliath, and he was the slingshot, or maybe even god.

Once our lunch arrived, it was placed on gold-rimmed plates embossed with the gold initials of the law firm. Our delicacy in this lap of luxury was from Subway. He didn't even pretend to hide it. Our food stared up at us still wrapped in the crinkly paper.

"Seems silly, doesn't it?" he quipped.

I nodded and released a bit of a chuckle. "Its a unique juxtaposition."

"After that many years without, I still always finish everything on my plate. It doesn't matter that I've eaten with presidents and kings, I always panic that I might not have a meal tomorrow. I guess it never really leaves you, does it? Poverty is a reality, but it is also a mindset."

TRUST IN ME

It did not matter that things were stabilizing. My father was never truly able to break free from the mentality of his own poverty. He was in constant survival mode. As the checks grew from his newfound consistent employment, so did our expenses. Things just didn't feel like they were getting better, even if in reality they were. And I was reaching my breaking point. The fear that this plane could crash any moment, shot down by unseen enemy fire, consumed me. It was too much and I decided I would rather jump and take my chances with the sharks below than wait around and trust that the engine wouldn't fail again.

Though Pensacola was not my scene, I began to build friendships and memories in the short year I had been here. I turned eighteen and my newly found best friend took me out to the beach with some of our theatre buddies where we howled at the moon and I kissed my time as a youth goodbye. I was entering into the full responsibility of legal adulthood. The choices I made from this point forward would no longer be expunged.

This shit mattered.

The week of my birthday brought with it many joys I never experienced before. This simple place had a unique tranquility to it that can only be captured in Jimmy Buffet lyrics.

I was finally experiencing some of the carefree feelings of youth that are often depicted in movies and soapy teen melodramas. I was making up for some lost time, but in that same notion, I desired deeply to get back on track to chase and catch my dreams. I was looking at my time in Pensacola as mere toleration, and my eighteenth birthday marked the moment where freedom would be mine. Finally, I could go my own way. Because with this moment … came a gift from the grave.

I arrived home from some of the festivities. Mom and Dad, apparently, had been waiting for me. They sat on the couch, notably separated. Nothing good ever comes from this obviously distant posturing. They informed me that this month had been really tight and they weren't sure how they would be able to pay all the bills. There was a way I could help, and, as I soon found out, I had actually already helped. The savings my grandfather had started for me in my childhood had been accessed by my father, who was a co-signer on the account. This had been used to alleviate whatever crisis was now happening. I had been given the honor of saving my family from falling back into homelessness.

With a statement like that, any anger or protestation I might have wanted to scream would have seemed like pure selfishness. Did I really want my family to end up living in motels, or worse, the streets?

I was assured that there was nothing to worry about. My father would pay me back by helping me get into a car. If I had been smarter, I would have questioned how it could make any level of sense that he could accomplish something like that if he had no money. But within a few weeks, he followed through on his promise. Sort of. He somehow got financed for a red Jeep Cherokee— the dream car of my adolescence. I should have asked how I would pay the remaining notes once he returned my non-consenting loan by making the initial payments for a few months. It's remarkable how stupid we can be when we are young.

My grandfather's dying gift, which was supposed to be an opportunity to truly start my life off in whatever direction I saw fitting at the time, became a means for my father to transfer his own cycle of poverty onto me. Though I was supposed to start my eighteenth year off in surplus, instead I began my adulthood in a debt I could not afford to maintain.

Less than a month from then, I would take a small knife out of my glove box and place the cold steel against my wrist. With steady determination, I pressed as hard against my natural instinct to live as I could. But the blade betrayed my depression and was too dull to make enough of an impact to end the misery inside me. Then, in a sudden moment of clarity, I decided there was an alternative to ending my freshman quarter at life.

In an act of criminal revenge, I stole my father's credit card and filled my tank with gas. My duffle bag packed in the back of the jeep, I capped the 80 MPH speedometer on my truck and blasted out of town, heading with all my might toward I-65. This was life or death. If I stayed with my family, I might never be able to break this circular poverty. I could find a better blade and cut so deep that I wouldn't be able to undo my permanent solution to a temporary situation. Or … I could fly. This jeep was the closest thing to pixie dust I had, and so I flew as fast as I could. I knew the way, first star on the right, and straight on 'til morning.

8. A Whole New World

"Adults are only kids grown up, anyway."
- Walt Disney

I Won't Say (I'm in Love)

For most people, the process of becoming a parent feels as if one day you are living a normal life, and the next day a baby is here, baptizing you into a new life. Your individualism suddenly disappears, replaced by the philosophy that many people describe as family, though that term is defined in different ways to different people. The time moves fast and the unique experience of pregnancy and childbirth becomes a distant memory, now replaced with the reality of diapers and midnight feedings. For me, fatherhood came much quicker than all that. It happened in an instant and it wasn't a decision I made. I was chosen by a little golden-haired princess.

I loved Tashina nearly the moment I saw her, but there was an added element of anxiety that came with our relationship. Though I had always been enamored with the idea of love, marriage, and family, for a young man in his early twenties, it was something that I had placed out in a distant future somewhere for when I grew up and had my shit together.

Now, as an adult who has lived more of this life, I realize that there is absolutely no amount of preparation that a person can do to truly be ready for parenthood. It doesn't matter if you are a teenage mother, a couple who planned for years, or someone preparing for an adoption or IVF. No matter which way a family is born, blended, or made, parenthood changes you. You can read every single blog, memorize volume one though a thousand of "What to Expect When You Are Expecting", and go to every single seminar on the subject, but in the end, the reality is that in some distinctive way, you are going to screw it all up.

Having been through my personal experience with my own family's poverty, I brought my own baggage into the anxiety of parenthood. I had created this mythology that somehow the pregnancy phase had hidden secrets within those nine months that would unleash the magic cure to fears about parenthood, and that with this newfound super knowledge, you wouldn't mess your own children up in the same way you felt wronged by your parents.

When it truly sank into my perpetually thick skull that the woman I loved had a child, I became increasingly distant. That feels absolutely horrible to say on this side of history, knowing my daughter now and having lived a life with this beautiful and amazing person who has changed me forever. Unlike many loving fathers who cuddle their precious newborn baby in their arms, moments after they are delivered, trying to say something wise while striking a pose for the grandparents, the first time I held my daughter, she was just "Tashina's kid." I stood there passively, minding my own business, when she asked me if I could help for "just a second" while she ran inside her apartment. With that, she handed me this squirming child and ran inside. You would think with as many sisters as I had, I wouldn't be afraid of a little baby, but I was absolutely terrified. Then again, siblings are a sub-species anyway. There I stood. Shocked. Holding this baby a full arms length away from my body, afraid that it would get baby all over me or something. Keep in mind that I still didn't have a fully developed frontal lobe at the time.

It is hard to believe that there was a time when I wasn't Kira's father, that for nearly the entire first year of her life, I was just a "sort of" boyfriend to her mother. The further we get from those original moments in our family's history, things have nearly been rewritten to place me in times where I certainly don't belong. It is hard not to do that with people we love. I even do that now with our other two children. It is almost impossible to imagine a world where they didn't exist, but one day they didn't, and then they did. Just like how I wasn't a father, until I was. Not because of anything I did, but because of the innocent love that only a child can truly posses. I didn't adopt Kira. She adopted me.

I have often said that Tashina and I never dated before we got married, and that is a very true statement. I had never taken her on a legitimate date, hadn't asked her to the movies, or out for a fancy dinner. Waffle House after a protest was the most romantic gesture I had ever mustered. Being parents now, my expectations of "alone time" and other things we take for granted in youth are silly notions, but Tashina already knew that, because by the time we met she was already a parent. However, we spent a different kind of quality time with each other, very much like we do now while being parents to three children. The difference was, in this scenario, I wasn't Dad yet. At least not in my mind. Little did I know that inside that baby brain of hers, she was putting together the pieces, and just as Tashina had already selected me as a life partner, little baby Kira had pegged me for another task altogether. She was slowly grooming me into a dad. I wasn't just being adopted, I was being adapted.

WHEN I SEE AN ELEPHANT FLY

Not all of the memories of my own childhood are negative. It wasn't all cold nights without electricity huddled around eating refried Ramen Noodles. Though my father failed in many ways, I see now that we all fall short in our attempts at parenting. It is absolutely impossible to know that from the vantage point of childhood. In the isolation of my own experience, it became all too easy to forget the times my father sat in our playroom and sculpted figurines with me or took us to swim at the local YMCA. Those memories became distant, another life altogether that existed outside of the prison of homelessness and despair that engulfed us.

I do not know the exact moment when I began to distrust my dad. After nearly a decade of hearing confessions of people who went through far more trauma at the hands of their parents than I ever experienced, I have learned that many people have isolated moments in time when a particular horrific event would sever relationships with their parents.

There is a moment in time that everything went south. Because of this, I always attempt to look at my own life in context. My father never laid a hand on my siblings or me. His faults lay far less in what he did, and more in what he didn't do. His own fight with poverty led him down a road of distancing himself emotionally and physically, which is a unique form of abuse all to its own that lends to a very different type of scarring.

For the first few years of our poverty, as we teetered on the precipice of homelessness, I truly believed my father when he would tell us that things would get better. In my mind, just beyond that hill we were climbing lay a valley, but far too often, it was just a larger hill that had to be climbed. This is not a condemnation, because I think that my father truly believed the hype he created. The more I have grown to know my father in adulthood, the more I realize that he genuinely believes that just beyond the horizon is his promise land. The older I get, the less bitter I have become for him being lost in the desert, and the more I find myself rooting for my father to win. In spite of my ability to forgive and even find these things endearing, that time of wandering weighed heavily on my childhood. I grew fatigued with what felt like a deception. Hope waned and gave way to a feeling that life would truly never get better.

I watched as my friends struggled with what I felt were normal adolescent issues, like being grounded or when parents would get them the wrong present for Christmas. In those moments, I thought about how much I would have loved nothing more than to trade problems with them. It was difficult to be a child when a world of adult level worries was carried on your shoulders. When my friends complained about their parents refusing to let them go out for a slumber party, it just seemed like a sitcom to me. Their fathers seemed like Bill Cosby or Tim Allen. Our life seemed like a subplot on Boston Public—a cautionary tale of the dangers of credit cards and having dreams.

It is easy to judge life in these microscopic ideologies when you are young. We don't see that instead of being the perfect dad, Bill Cosby is actually drugging young women and sexually assaulting them. So I wouldn't trade my life and experiences for someone else's. That is the danger in covertness. We cannot judge someone's experiences based upon outward facades of perfection. There are unspeakable crimes upon innocence happening in the suburbs, just as there are to children living on the streets, but the narcissism of childhood led me to believe that my life was unique and that I was the only person in the world with a father inept enough to allow us to fall so low as to be living in fear of where we would stay each night.

The fears I collected along our family's journey would carry with me. I did not want my children, should I ever choose to have them, to grow up in the type of world that I had lived in. I didn't want them to have a father who was so busy worrying about feeding them that he couldn't eat with them. My journey to prevent my ideological future children from that life would lead me on a path to become someone fighting not only to prevent that for myself, but for countless other children.

JUST AROUND THE RIVER BEND

In the earliest times of our bizarre courtship, Tashina and I spent most of our free nights at protests or social events with other activists, instead of fancy dinners. We were changing the world. What could a relaxing dinner do to change that? It seemed I was also too busy to have dinner with the family. Pensacola was on the verge of something, but what that something was, well, it was sometimes hard to tell. Some days it felt like it would either be a cultural renaissance or maybe a civil war. In the end, it was hard to decide.

Cleaning up a decaying community can bring about ripe opportunities for social injustice.

It is difficult to find the balance of knowing that there needs to be economic growth while also ensuring that others aren't crushed by the weight of progress. I became a frustrating anomaly to both the power structures within our community and amongst activists. The city council would become angry with me for pointing out that tent cities would be destroyed by development, but the activists would look at me as a traitor for helping relocate the camp sites, instead of chaining myself to trees. However, having been homeless myself, I was unwilling to use the poor as props in social unrest. Some child's future rested on their father getting a job selling hotdogs inside the ball park that was going to be built on top of the waterfront property that was once the Badlands.

I was quickly becoming a liaison between those living in poverty and the power brokers of our small town. There is absolutely no way to be a voice of the downtrodden and not step on a few dozen important toes along the way. Occasionally, my outspokenness would land me at odds with neighborhood associations, special interests, or the occasional oddball who considered his or herself far more important then they really were.

One evening we were in the middle of a battle over an issue and when I arrived home an email awaited me, explaining that this person would kill me. They had gone into extreme detail about the place and manner in which they would do it. At our community picnic for the homeless. The very next day. If I arrived to distribute food to the hundreds of poor men, women, and children who counted on us, then this guy would put a bullet in my head.

For half a moment, I thought about what a cruel irony it would be that I had survived my family's poverty and then might very well die relieving someone else's hunger. It seemed like a no brainer that I would go. What kind of activist would I be if I allowed some whacko with a Judas complex to terrorize me away from doing the right thing?

That night, I called Tashina and asked her if she would meet me at a small park by the water. I told her about everything—the email and what it said. I also explained why it was important that I go. Maybe other women would have tried to talk a man out of walking into the line of fire. People often accused me of being full of piss and vinegar, and that was true. And still is. What they seldom see is that normally those ingredients are supplied to me by that woman. I suppose other men might have been insulted, like she was trying to get rid of me or something, but in that moment I knew she really loved me. She understood me.

"You know, if this guy doesn't shoot me tomorrow, I have every intention to marry you."

"I know."

And with that, she kissed me. It was hardly a proposal, just a confession. If I was going to die, she might as well know that I had planned to get over my fear of living the rest of my life with her. As it would turn out, the guy never did shoot me dead. My newfound lease on life did not cause me to run to the altar or anything. There was plenty more hard-to-get to be played, and I had accidentally went and showed my ace. But Kira was concocting her own plan to woo my heart. She just had to learn how to talk first.

"All cartoon characters and fables must be exaggeration, caricatures. It is the very nature of fantasy and fable."- Walt Disney

Poor Unfortunate Souls

Cynical people tend to complain about fairytales, mistakenly accusing them of creating a false sense of reality. I will admit that they typically have fairy godmothers, talking animals, and finite villains. However, the critics of fairytale storytelling models tend to overlook the realities that are in no way embellished about the fables. Even the fabricated bits are based in some form of reality, at least in the hyper-condensed sense. Fairy godmothers, for example, represent all of the people who come together in our lives and make miracles happen. For the point of narrative, one magical creature or person is created in order to

113

quickly resolve all of life's conflicts with the shake of a wand. The fairy godmother is the social worker, pastor, kind gas station attendant, and taxi cab driver who gives you free fare, all wrapped up into one person. Just like the villain tends to make up everyone from your high school bully, malicious family member, and employer who lets you go right before Christmas, all in an easily hated form.

In real life, no person is all good or bad. But sometimes the bad that someone does, or in equal measure the good, can leave such a lasting impact that they can only be understood in those hyperbolic terms. I mean, I am sure that at some point, Hitler helped a kitty out of a tree or a grandmother cross the road, but who really gives a shit because he is arguably the most condensed version of evil the world has ever known. So it is completely possible, in spite of your good, to truly become a villain unworthy of redemption, even in real life.

Thankfully, few of us will ever interact with a cruel genocidal dictator in our lifetime. But when we are forced to explain the struggles of our lives— childhood abusers, landlords that evicted us, family or friends who have abandoned us, or worse, propelled us into the darkness that is now driving our life—how do we explain their existence? Evil? Devil?

Villain.

It is all very real and for the less believable bits, like pixie dust and flying carpets, they are just hope. These things represent our dreams and ambitions. They help us to soar high into the sky of possibility when everything seems lost. When life has reached its cruelest moments, when the villain is standing over us without rescue in sight, we can close our eyes, think a happy thought, and hold tight onto hope in whatever form it might be coming.

Without hope, what do we have left?

The engagement portion of the relationship with my partner was definitely like a fairytale. Not the glass slipper, gold carriage, and ornate wedding in a castle part. No. In the really bad family politics kind of way. Just like in the classic stories, both of our families had ideas of what they wanted their children to become and who they would marry. I certainly didn't feel like we were a dynasty worthy of post-adulthood parental oversight, but apparently I was wrong. It seemed like everyone had an opinion about our nuptials.

This is the part of life where mythology and fairytale betray reality in the worst way. Tashina wasn't a virgin. Now, that wasn't something folks generally would be able to do much more than speculate and gossip about, but Kira was this walking, talking, say-yes-to-the-off-white-dress kind of sign.

Apparently, finding love was not enough. All aspects of life had to be perfect and chaste. I would be lying if I said I did not have my own reservations, but what I grew to realize is that they weren't actually my reservations at all, they were my parents'. And arguably, they weren't my parents' either, but society's. The churches we had gone to had built up this amazing fable about virginity, which is really just a bizarre myth created by a patriarchal society in order to control and dictate female sexuality, but I digress. The religious context of my early life was rearing its ugly head and demanding something more than love from our relationship.

I highly doubt that at the end of The Notebook, Noah curled up on that nursing room bed with Ally and as the camera pulled away, whispered in her ear, "I loved you for decades, read you stories so you would remember our love since you began to lose your memory, just so that we could have moments of clarity like this one, and I know we are dying in each others arms and all ... but I really wish you hadn't slept with Cyclops."

Even though I was doing everything I could do to be like an actual adult and realize that it's really none of my business what Tashina did with her life before I came along, it was pretty much all anyone in my family could think about. It was like Kira was the punctuation mark at the end of the "your wife is a whore" sentence. Now, that sentence was normally veiled behind other remarks. Like when my brother sat me down and said, "Tashina has a darkness about her. There is something evil about that girl, I hate to break it to you." This is a highlighted example of how personal perspective can be so very wrong.

We were trying desperately to do everything we could to learn how to be a family in spite of it all. She was coming with the luggage of a toddler, a previous courtroom marriage, the loss of her mother, and daddy issues. I was bringing the U-

Haul full of poverty, fear, and guilt baggage. So, like most completely dysfunctional adults, we decided to raise children together.

A Very Merry Christmas Party

We decided to open the shelter full-time starting on Christmas Eve. There just seemed to be something poetically damning about the thought of potentially turning homeless families away on the day we remember there being no room for Mary and baby Jesus. I think even an atheist's skin would crawl if they did something like that. Even though, at the time, in my own spiritual journey, I was stuck somewhere between reformed religious zealot and devoting my soul to Christopher Hitchins. I just couldn't escape the feeling that there was going to be something really special about this night.

A young family rolled up to our front door, both of the babies asleep in the car, and they were looking for a safe place to stay. We had only one room left and they took it. Christmas time was full of chaos. Presents flooded in, people from all over the community made decadent dishes for dinner, and gift cards were given for the parents to be able to buy things they needed. The love and support was profound. On Christmas Eve, we had a difficult time scheduling folks to volunteer for the overnight shift because of holiday plans. However, in a beautiful moment of seasonal magic, two volunteers came forward—one being Jewish and the other Muslim—so that those who celebrated

Christmas could celebrate with family. That is the profound power found in coming together for a common cause that transcends theology.

After dinner, I sat down to talk with our newest family. They had two young children, one was almost three and the other a newborn. They had traveled from Chicago to the heart of the south to witness a loved one's wedding. They had been struggling financially and a family member offered to help with gas if they would just come. There was one minor detail that the young mother had left out. Her husband was Hispanic. Her family absolutely lost their minds over the subject.

Needless to say, they weren't able to get the gas money from their bigoted cousin. This led to not being able to make it back to their home in time and jobs were lost. They were spiraling into the snarly teeth of homelessness and that evil beast was ready to swallow them whole. In a moment of desperation, they contacted the police department and one of the officers took them in for a brief time, and finally, they arrived to spend some time with us at the shelter.

One of our volunteers set up a special job fair with the local hotel chains, and soon they were able to find employment. Another agency that we partnered with helped them with other issues that had to be resolved to help them achieve full-time housing. A local hairdresser even gave the wife a mini-makeover to boost her self-esteem. By the time winter was over, they had a new-to-them vehicle, a house, and employment. It was a beautiful thing to witness. Their family had acted cruelly and kicked them off the edge of the poverty cliff, all because of prejudice.

At the end of life, this story will become condensed, and the dozens of people who helped participate in their success will likely become lost to the annals of time. By the time the stories are told and retold, the details will be forgotten. Someone will ignore the part this couple played in their own success, or our volunteers advocating on their behalf to find employment, or the compassionate police officer who took a convict in because it was Christmas. Those details will become absorbed by time and storytelling, and likely a legend will be born. One where one individual will receive the bulk of the credit and will become a fairy godmother who fixed all the problems with a bibbity-bobbity-boo. But I know the truth is that everyone participates in order for true success to take place and that even the simplest deed can make a huge impact. I know that the magic wand isn't dainty and sleek. It weighs a few tons of human flesh willing to move mountains and shout down injustice.

THEY'RE FINALLY GETTING MARRIED

It isn't sex or the hocus pocus of vows that makes you a parent. Any bozo with the proper equipment can become a parent. There is no talent to bringing a child into the world. However, being a mother or father is a totally different idea all together. Tashina and I were learning from each other, about parenting, about running a household together. We were placing a measly savings together, hoping for a beautiful wedding.

We were practical people, even back then, and so there were just certain things we knew were out of the question. We would not be having a massive catered reception, but we had hoped to make it to Disney World for our honeymoon. It seemed like a romantic notion to mark the real beginning of my adulthood by completing a childhood dream. Our original plan was to be married in an old historic church downtown. It was so part of the plan that it was where I had originally proposed to her. I said, "If we ever got married, you are certain this is the place?" And when she nodded a shy affirmation, I fell to one knee and asked her if she would marry me right there. However, we would neither be married nor honeymoon at our original destinations of choice.

Life and family conflicts kept pushing our wedding date back. We had originally hoped for a fall date, but some rift within my family made that event impossible if we wanted everyone to be there to witness our wedded bliss. Finally, our car broke down in a moment of anti-karma. We broke into the piggy bank and what would have been three nights at the Animal Kingdom Lodge, magically morphed into a busted green Jeep Cherokee.

It finally became clear to us that our little family that was being pieced together did not harmonize with the hopes and ambitions of Tashina's Lady Tramaine and my King Triton, respectively. We could keep pushing back wedding dates and promise not to have alcoholic beverages served at the reception, but not a single one of those things would sew Tashina's virginity back together, and it sure as hell wasn't going to somehow make us any more ready to be parents. Nothing ever does. So, since we had no control over other people's reactions to our life choices, we decided to elope in style.

We gave out little invitations to close friends and family, announcing that in two weeks' time we would gather in a local park and exchange vows under a white-washed cross that had been there for ages. We just decided it was time for the world to recognize what we already knew. We were basically Brangelina, and therefore unstoppable. All of the experiences that resulted from our semi-rebellious decision to just get married made it all worth it.

Wedding dresses and tuxedos go out of style, parents have a funny way of getting over things as the grandchildren start to role in, and basically nothing about a wedding day goes as planned. But that isn't the point of a wedding. Lots of people in this world will get married just to have the experience of a wedding. Some couples will become so caught up in the planning that they stop being couples, and instead become business partners attempting to close an acquisition. We decided to skip that part and just be married because it was what would be best for us and for our way of expressing it.

Did we live happily ever after? Well, our lives don't begin or end at the altar. So I can't tell you if this moment is the happiest, and most ever-ist experience of our entire life together or apart. What

I can say is that prejudice never does anyone any good. It costs us memories, and even if we grow past these dark moments, it leaves scars.

As we were lost in our own melodrama of marriage, there were laws being challenged. But these laws didn't prevent princesses from marrying paupers. They prevented people from being able to choose who they wanted to marry, based solely upon a personal interpretation of sacred text. If life had been different, we likely would have chosen not to get married, and simply reside with each other in love. If nothing else, to stand in solidarity with the thousands of others who were being barred from exchanging vows legally. Our own families' rejection of our love helped create a context for us to soon fight for others to be able to make their own decisions about whom they wanted to marry.

But that could all wait. We had a honeymoon to get to. Disney would have to wait for another day, another event. That, however, did not spoil one bit our time together that weekend.

10. LET IT GO

"All our dreams can come true, if we have the courage to pursue them."- Walt Disney

FIXER UPPER

If we truly boil it down, life is made up of two parts. Things that we do on purpose and things that happen to us. Getting or losing a job is something that happens. So is starting a business, meeting someone new on the subway, your unit being called off to war, being diagnosed with cancer, or being in a catastrophic car accident. These moments just happen. Some people attribute them to a divine or evil force. We call them serendipitous, karma, freaks of nature. What we do with these moments can change everything. I have met soldiers from the Vietnam War, both were drafted, both didn't believe in the war, both ended up homeless because of poor policies under the

Reagan administration. One never stopped fighting and he eventually got the money he was entitled to, with back pay. The other guy just gave up on expecting those in power to follow though. The first guy finally moved into a house, got a bed, and had a safe place to live for the first time in decades. He died in his sleep six months later. The other guy still lives on the streets of Pensacola and is one of the happiest people I have ever met. I don't even pretend to have life figured out anymore, but I sure am enjoying the ride.

In my social advocacy work, this has been the hardest point to drive home to people who think they have it all figured out. You ask the average citizen and they will tell you exactly how to fix the "problem" of homelessness. Each time I have these conversations, I am constantly glad that I am the professional, and that they are an accountant somewhere.

I do not believe that everyone has to be the CEO of a Fortune 500 company in order to be happy. Arguably, I have met more happy people in homeless camps than I have at business meetings, but that is for another book. The point is that life happens to you, and sometimes you have to make some big choices that can make all the difference. Sometimes that means you risk everything you have in order to produce a cutting edge full length cartoon, and other times that means that you just realize that you've gotta make the best of the mess.

When I made the decision to be a dad, I decided to go in headfirst. I am the type of person that just sort of does things first, but instead of ask forgiveness, I just explain why you were wrong and I was brilliant and you just missed it. That isn't the easiest lifestyle to maintain, but there is never a dull moment in my head. That being said, there is also rarely a dull moment around me, because the things I think inside my head don't stay there long. But I began to realize that this ideology, though it helped me get the job done in the world of activism, was not necessarily the best parenting technique. Responding to, "Daddy, why is the sky blue?" with, "To hell if I know, read a science book, or better yet stop having moments of existential crisis and start worrying about the fact that there is a 10% unemployment rate and fix the problems within your immediate community. Once you deal with that, then you will have all the time in the world to wonder why the sky is blue," is basically the worst way to be a parent.

I was going to need some help.

Fortunately, one of my mentors growing up was a child psychologist. He was the best kind of child psychologist possible. He was one of the volunteers at our local community theatre and his big event every year was to put on a Haunted House fundraiser for the programs there. It was a huge success every year, with lines wrapping around the block. One day, my best friend and I cornered the good doctor and asked him if he felt like a hypocrite scaring the ever living shit out of children all day. He looked at us with a cold and serious expression on his face, "Boys, this is job security. Their parents pay me to break them and then pay me to fix them. This is just good business." I am pretty sure he was joking, but you get the general picture that this guy is amazing. So a few weeks before my wife and I were married, I took the doc out to lunch.

I sat with him and let my guard down. I just unloaded everything. I was beginning to see why the guy was so good at his job. He just had one of those personalities that made you want to unravel everything. I knew fellow priests that were like that. They were like confession vampires that could just suck every last drop of your craziness out and you walked away feeling all born again and stuff. Well, that was what was happening here. I just couldn't stop talking in dizzying circles about my fears and anxieties about being a parent. What was I supposed to do if she ended up wanting to move in with her bio-dad at fifteen? What if she hates me? What am I supposed to do if I yell or scream or drop her on her head? He just sat across from me, expressionless, taking it all in.

"Ok, so do you wanna know the truth or would you rather that I just say something nice that will make you feel better, since you are buying lunch?" He said it with no sense of irony at all. It was literally a red pill/blue pill type moment.

I said I wanted to know the truth.

"Here is the deal. You are going to screw your kids up. There is absolutely not a damn thing you can do to avoid it. You can be the most amazing liberal parent on the planet, and your kids will become entitled little shits running around spending all your money and won't move out until they finally sell all your memories once you are dead. Or you can take the other approach and be a fascist level conservative and never let them leave the house and they will just dig out of the house with a spoon. Basically, you cannot avoid messing this whole thing up. What you have to decide is in what way do you wanna screw them up? Trying really hard to be an amazing parent or by disconnecting? All you can do is try."

"That's it?"

"Oh, and listen. If she wants to take your last name, she will tell you. If she wants to call the other guy Dad, she will. Just let her be her own person. The more you listen and only get involved when it's something that is actually life or death, the happier you both will be."

With that, I paid our tab and off he rode off into the sunset of awesome adults from my childhood. It was the best $12.73 I had ever spent.

FRIENDS ON THE OTHER SIDE

There is a crucial point in the moment of poverty where it transitions over into homelessness. The landlord is banging on the door and demanding your full rent or he will file official eviction papers. You only have $200 dollars. So you can A) Hold onto the money and hope for the best, maybe an agency will finally call you back, B) Blow it on lotto tickets, probably have better chances with this then the agency calling you back, especially since it's the end of the month, C) Invest in that little start up business you always wanted to, or D) Treat yourself family to the absolutely best dinner they've ever had, because tomorrow is going to be a really rough day.

My parents had different coping mechanisms to deal with the struggles we faced. Though you could never be sure what my father's was, and sometimes it would be rather fluid. Some days I couldn't tell if Dad was buying himself a Starbucks because he just landed a gig, or because, "Screw it, that last four dollars wouldn't have changed a thing about my situation."

Though my father couldn't really be pegged, Mom wore her emotions on her sleeve. That is not entirely accurate, she also wore her emotions on everyone else's sleeve within a one-mile radius. Mom felt a great deal of emotions. There was a lot going on there. Some days, she would be optimistic about our hypothetical future, defending my father as her best friend and lover. Other days, she sat in her room watching While You Were Sleeping on repeat, cursing the day she met him. It was a bit baffling to watch as a child. Dad, who seemed completely disconnected emotionally, and Mom, who had enough emotions for an entire village. I am pretty sure Tammy Faye Bakker was her spirit animal.

We were living in the house at the end of a winding road and Mom was really into prophets at the time. I suppose the whole idea of a prosperity gospel had become her version of the lottery. Sometimes, people would drop money into the offering plate and they would be healed or receive a random check in the mail and life would get better for them. At least that's what was always in the promotional videos of the latest up and coming new prophet of God. Most weekends we would attend prophetic gatherings at the TBN Headquarters right outside of downtown Nashville. The shows were spectacular! It was like David Copperfield, except with Jesus, and everyone believes it is real.

One week, the top five coolest prophets of the age where hosting this mega meeting in Orlando, Florida. My mom asked me to go with her. I would be lying if I said that, to my teenage mind, I hoped that some of this was true. I wished that God thought about me as much as I thought about him, and that I was special. That maybe he would speak through some guy to talk to me. Knowing that there might be a plan for all of this chaos could be enough to go on for just one more day.

We drove the whole way and we could tell we were close to Orlando when the telephone lines changed into Mickey Mouse ears. We drove in swirls along the interstate, finally arriving at the church, but it was clear that there was a mouse overshadowing the sentiment of the moment.

"Wouldn't it be nice to go one day?" Mom said with a whimsical sound that was normally reserved only for church.

"Yeah, it would be Mom."

"We will go. Things are going to get better. God will come through. You've just got to believe it."

With that, we went inside. The music was loud and chaotic, the prophets selected people from the crowd like it was a John Edwards Show. "There is a man with a red shirt." "Someone knows someone who has cancer." And amazingly, there was always a guy with a red shirt, and without fail, there was always someone who really did know another person who had cancer that desperately needed healing. Who doesn't? However, standing in rooms amongst thousands of people, these are hardly miracles. It is just people who desperately want to believe in the fairytale. They are looking for their fairy godmother, and instead find Dr. Fallacier. Just drop a couple of dollars in the plate and maybe you will win the luck of the draw. They've got friends on the other side.

God did not speak to us that week, even though we traveled hundreds of miles. With each word, we craned our necks and sat close to the front, hoping to be noticed by God. I don't know why God would have an easier time spotting us in the front, but we were trying really hard for God to notice. Mom even fasted one day in order to be able to put a whole $20 dollar bill in the offering plate. Apparently, there were more pressing issues for the deity to attend to.

As we drove away, Mom had that same look in her eyes that the guy who buys scratch offs has when he just knows that the next one is the winner. He drops another dollar. The reality that neither scratch off guy or my mom could see is that if they just saved that dollar each time, maybe they would be able to buy whatever it is that they think they might get if they win. But they won't do that, and that is why the lottery makes billions of dollars and that guy is poor. Maybe if everyone just stopped dropping money in the offering plate, and instead pulled it all together, they could pay for the woman sitting in the front to get eye surgery and then she wouldn't be blind anymore. I mean, it's not as flashy as a guy with perfect white teeth putting on the show, but it smells a whole lot more like Jesus then it does like bullshit.

As we pulled away from the church, no winnings to show for it, she looked out into the distance, "I wonder if we could see the castle."

I told her that I doubted it, but the entire time as we drove away from Orlando, I looked above the trees. Maybe I would see it, and maybe Tinkerbell would fly across the sky and the music would fade, and everything would be better. For now, I was just going to have to believe that it would all get better one day and that Dad would follow through on his promise.

This was the litmus test, the finish line to prove that everything was finally going to be all right and that we had made it through the wilderness. But, soon the telephone lines turned back to normal. I knew in that moment that my dad wasn't going to take my siblings and I on our epic family vacation, because things weren't going to get better. I knew it because my mom just paid for some man's Lexus instead of paying our car payment. These guys weren't the fairy godmothers everyone needed them to be. They were the Wizard of Oz. And it was past time for the curtain to fall.

Tashina, Kira, and I drove into Orlando and there were those same telephone lines I had been waiting to see again since I was that wayward and faith-filled teenager. The genesis of the three of us being here was a series of very real choices and no prophet was necessary. My sister-in-law was getting married in Tampa. This was a required event to attend and we were given a six-month warning so that my wife could buy shoes and a dress. That was also enough time to make some other very special plans.

Something you need to know about Tashina is that she has a dangerously adventurous spirit. If she ever won that lottery mentioned above, she would travel the world six times over and still be unsatisfied, knowing there was still more world to see out there. She is so full of wanderlust that even the simplest tasks can become overwhelming. If I recommend a weekend trip to New Orleans, which is a short drive away, the next thing I know, she has itemized our departure budget based upon estimation of gas and food consumption, breaking down at least sixteen other locations I could take her on the same dime.

When she agreed to be the matron of honor in her sister's wedding, this same mechanism kicked in. She looked at me with a solemn determination.

"We are going to Disney World," she said matter-of-factly.

Both Kira and I looked up from our fixated gaze at whatever book we were reading. Tashina had an entire breakdown set before us. She printed out a map of Magic Kingdom and a savings sheet of how much money we would have to put aside over the next six months in order to be able to afford one day park tickets and to pay for the extra gas. If we arrived at the park at opening and stayed until closing, we could ride every single ride that Kira's little stature would allot.

The next few months became a whirlwind of actions of will. We didn't eat out. Three times a week the three of us went to the mall and walked in circles so Kira could adapt to extra walking. We prepared like a militia for the task ahead of us. We would conquer Disney World and we only had one day to do it.

The day finally arrived. Princess dress, check. Mickey ears, check. Snacks, check. We loaded up the van and made the short drive from Tampa straight into Disney World. The sky was perfect. Small puffy clouds hovered in front of the perfectly blue sky. I couldn't help but think that it looked exactly like Andy's wallpaper. Kira exclaimed as the signs appeared, welcoming us to the park.

We parked, we walked, and we arrived on the boat. There it was, just over the waterway. I could feel Tashina's reassuring hand on my back, "You've made it, honey. We are here." Only she truly understood the significance of this moment. However, I was not ready to relax just yet. My life had been faced with too much disappointment, this moment was too profound, and I just had to be certain. I told her I wouldn't believe it until I was through the gates. I stood there, almost like stone, just staring at the castle as it grew larger while the waves lapped against the side of the boat. It was like the home I had envisioned in my mind when we had none. This was an affirmation of my childhood belief that Cinderella really could rise up from the ashes and that you truly could come from nothing and make a difference.

Could dreams really come true?

The boat docked. We unloaded. They carefully checked our bags and we handed them our passes.

We were in.

Kira walked up and took my hand. She stood there with me pointing down Main Street, USA, past the concessions and candies, past the balloons, past Walt and Mickey taking a very similar pose, and there it was.

Cinderella's Castle.

And here was my beautiful little princess standing there with me. An uncontrollable tear formed in my eye.

Without a shadow of a doubt, I knew in that moment that I would fail as a father. Just like the good doctor told me, I would screw this whole thing up no matter how hard I tried. But no matter what I did, from this moment forward, the mistakes I made would be my own mistakes. The sins I commit would be my own, not my father's.

I had broken the cycle.

It would be a poor man's vacation. It would be rushed and sweaty. We would miss so many magical things on that first visit, but it did not matter. We were here.

Dreams really do come true.

11. Part of Your World

"The way to get started is to quit talking and begin doing."- Walt Disney

Oo-De-Lally (Walking Through the Forest)

The word homeless covers a great many sins. What people say when they use the word homeless, and the realities that come along with that word, are very different. Growing up, my experience was as far removed from racial disparity generational poverty as it was from the struggles of the chronic homeless man flying a sign for UFO parts. Yes, we are all struggling with the same systemic issue of lack of adequate housing, but the causes aren't the same. Cancer sucks and it kills you, but the struggles of a child with leukemia and a chronic smoker dying of rotting lungs are apples and oranges. Now, I don't despise the chronic smoker for his decisions. He has been systematically preyed upon by an industry that has purposefully played into the disease of addiction. In a similar way, though some might choose to blame a person for their personal struggles with poverty and homelessness, it is important to remember that personal responsibility ends where systematic oppression begins.

When people refuse to acknowledge that differences exist within the header of that title of homeless, it creates many societal issues. There is only one cure for homelessness and that is, quite simply, having a home. It does not matter if you are a family who found yourself without a home due to a fire or a war vet mainlining heroin under an overpass, what will fix your homelessness is having a home. It truly is that simple. The genuine simplicity of the conceptual solution is mind boggling for some people. Instantly, emotions flare about cost, which is also simple. It costs three times as much to arrest someone for homeless related "crimes", as it would to just give them a home.

Though the cure for homelessness is universal, the ways to prevent future homelessness are not. Some are simple, like raising the minimum wage so that people can actually afford to live in houses while working one forty hour a week job. Other solutions are more complicated, like never sending people into senseless wars that can't be won, which slowly decreases their morale. All the while refusing to give them proper medical treatment, breaking them mentally and emotionally, and then saluting with a, "Thanks for your service," while dropping them off at the local rescue mission.

Knowing and understanding the causes and effects of homelessness can help prevent people from ending up on the streets from the start. This is also a substantially less expensive idea. The amount of money it costs to stop a vet from ending up on the streets by providing basic mental health care, for example, is far cheaper than arresting him for basic human needs that instantly become illegal once you end up on the streets, such as sleeping or using the restroom in public.

Living in motels because your parents can't find work is not the same as the children I meet weekly who are literally born into homelessness. It is also alarmingly different than the street life of the chronically homeless. Each comes with its own struggles, stigma, and challenges. The only way to end it is housing, but the means by which we create the access to housing is truly dependent upon the circumstances. These are nuanced situations that need real time case management and access to resources. Not political grandstanding.

When I first decided that I wanted to work alongside those currently affected by homelessness, I knew that I didn't completely understand what that meant. I realized that the experience of the chronic male population was truly different from my own experience with homelessness growing up. I needed to understand the gap—what was different and what was the same. So I decided to do what any rational thinking twenty-something did: live as the street homeless do for a few weeks.

There now exists a trend that is rather disturbing. It's called "homeless tourism" and it's when people of means take a day, week, or month to live as the poor. These experiences are very different from other forms of supposedly "choosing" homelessness that is experienced by the train hoppers and beach rat runaways. When Tashina ran away from her home and affluence as a teenager, that is not a type of poverty appropriation, that is becoming impoverished for survival. When someone chooses to leave their privilege for a weekend, that does not make them homeless and it cannot bring true understanding, even if it does bring some level of awareness. The genuine fear, loss of self-esteem, and depression that comes with being the forgotten of society is unable to be comprehended in a 48-hour time period, no matter how scared you might have been to sleep on a sidewalk.

However, in life's truest poetic sense, it was not until I had finally given up on my little walkabout that the enlightenment I sought was found.

The original plan was to walk from Pensacola and slowly make my way up to Chicago, unsure if I would go further. I hadn't really thought that part out. All that I did know is that I wanted to experience one of the facets of homelessness that I didn't understand. So, I stayed in shelters, slept on church doorsteps, and let strangers buy me food. But like most things in life, it wasn't when I was trying to learn that I was given the lesson I needed. It wasn't until I diverted off the path that the road became straight.

Instead of making it all the way along my journey, I became distracted by a pretty girl during a pit stop in Nashville. Home has a funny way of always reeling you back in. It will use any tactic necessary, be it pleasure or pain. If a job promotion won't bring you back, maybe a family tragedy will. Life is cruel and kind all at once.

One day, I got the bug to go to church. I think most young Christian mini-adults have a built in calendar that sends off warning signs that it's been a couple of weeks too long since you last attended a service, just to make sure you never backslide. Whatever my personal reason might have been that night, I never actually made it inside the church building. This particular congregation was in the heart of downtown in a building that used to be a Planet Hollywood. It had a pristine coffee shop and they rented it out as a venue during the week. I made it up to the front of the door and read the sign that was posted, "PRIVATE EVENT." Before I even had the opportunity to really wrap my mind around the theological dilemma this concept was, I heard a request booming from a large deep voice behind me.

"Hey, bud. Can you spare some change?"

I turned around to see a scruffy old man sitting on one of the cement planters, which encircled a tree in the middle of the concrete sidewalk. He didn't smile and judging by the number of functional teeth he had, it was probably a good sales technique not to. I told him apologetically that I didn't have any money.

"Well, how about a cigarette then?"

I looked into the church through the large glass doors, watching as people ordered their lattes and gathered in beautiful little clusters. I would have fit in there. My teeth were almost white enough, my hair was thick and ice tipped, my pants and shoes passed the grade. Sure, I couldn't sing and my manners could use some improving, but I made a decent enough match for this congregation. The man sitting at my feet asking for a cigarette, he was likely the reason that this event was private. Even though I could walk right through these doors with zero fear of oppression, the line that separated this man and myself was very thin. It all depends on how you categorize homelessness.

In that moment I made a decision and it was one that would forever alter my course. What is funny about these types of moments is that rarely do they feel very important. There are certainly moments where you can feel the weight of their significance —the moment you see the person you will spend the rest of your life with or when you make the decision to be a parent—but this didn't feel at all like that. I simply turned around and handed a cigarette to a guy wanting to bum one. What harm could there possibly be in that? Well, other than cancer and heart disease.

But three hours and one pack of cigarettes later, it was clear that everything was different. He introduced himself as Bear. That was his call name in the military. He had fought in Vietnam and told me about how he fell though the cracks of bureaucracy during the Reagan administration. Though there existed countless entitlements for former military, legislation made it increasingly more difficult to apply for and receive these benefits. So here he was on cold cement begging on Main Street, USA.

He explained that all he wanted to do in this world was make an honest dollar and have a place that he could call home. "Kid, anywhere that means I don't wake up with some goddamn cop flashing a light in my face. That's my heaven. I don't need golden streets, just to not end up taking an unintended golden shower because some drunk pisses on me in the middle of the night."

Bear was a grunt and rude. He was leathered from the war he fought overseas and the one he was fighting here at home. One of his eyes barely opened, like he was constantly making a Clint Eastwood impression, but there was a warmth about him and his stories that compelled me toward action.

In a few days I would be leaving for Pensacola to visit my family. A hurricane had just hit and there was a great deal of work, construction, and clean up while the town was rebuilding itself. Maybe Bear could rebuild himself too. It was the closest thing to a land of milk and honey I could create. I sort of blurted out the invitation and he accepted. We made arrangements to meet at the same location on the day I was leaving town.

As I finished my shift that day, a sense of nervousness filled me. Part of me sort of hoped that he wouldn't be there waiting for me, but there he stood waiting by a stop sign. Was this a warning from Jesus? Likely, I thought. However, I had made a commitment and I intended to keep it. He looked less intimidating in the daylight, the way an alley seems more inviting, but the sun was quickly setting.

On our journey south, he pulled off his muddied old boots and put his feet up. He reflected on how this was the first time he had felt like he could relax in a long time, and with that, he fell fast asleep. As his snores and the scent of decaying feet filled the air, I looked over at the gruff guest sleeping next to me. All of a sudden I realized he had a glaring resemblance to Charles Manson. I was suddenly gripped with a sense of fear and stupidity. I didn't read the newspaper or own a TV. For all I knew, I had just picked up a serial killer. Fantastic. Well, at least it would make for a hell of a punch line to an obituary.

Not in Nottingham

When Tashina, Kira, and I returned home from our one-day Disney extravaganza, I couldn't help but realize how different it was from other experiences. Often, things we build up in our mind, like Christmas day or a first date, fall short of our expectations. The magic that existed within that island was real. Though we were saturated within that joy while there, upon returning to the real world I was stricken with an odd sense of guilt. I didn't want to even discuss the topic of our trip with my father or my siblings.

My feelings of elation of rising above the perceived failures of my father hardly seemed like coffee table conversation with the man whom I felt that I had overcome. Was I supposed to discuss with him how it felt as if my childhood had been redeemed in a certain sense? How would that be taken? As much as I blamed my father for these things, in some ways correctly and in others absurdly, I certainly didn't want to cause him harm. Hurting another person because of your pain never makes a situation better, no matter how gratifying it may feel in the moment.

When my father did finally call, it was instantly awkward. My strained "hello" seemed laced with, "Hey, I took Kira to Disney and it was awesome and amazing and wonderful, and basically everything I ever thought it would be and then some. You ruined my childhood."

Then the dreaded question came.

"How was Disney?"

The truth is, it was magical and was made more so because it was a mountain top moment for me. I needed my dad to see that, I needed him to understand that just because our childhood was difficult, that doesn't mean that I hated him (even if at certain points in my youth I had literally said, "I hate you for this." What I really meant was, "I am scared and I really hate this situation, and I blame you, which is partially fair, and I just need to you to acknowledge that and let me be a kid and not expect more of me than is reasonable.") Nothing about this conversation was going to be easy, that is unless I just avoided the reality within myself.

"It was good, Dad."

Clearly, that wasn't the best explanation. I was going to need to come up with more than that. But what? That it was amazing running up and down the streets of Magic Kingdom hand in hand with Kira? That Mickey gave me a hug and I cried? That the food really wasn't that expensive? Really, we just split meals because we couldn't even eat a whole veggie burger there anyway. And to be honest, you spent more money buying domain names for online businesses you'd never start than it cost for us to buy one-day tickets.

I was really having a hard time with this.

"Were there any highlights?"

I wanted to say, "Yes, Dad. Splash Mountain was absolutely amazing. And we threw our hands up in the air and in the photo we looked just like the families in the commercials. No, I don't think that this means I won't screw up in certain ways, but it is my step towards forging my own path in this life and I am just trying to figure out what the hell it means to be a dad. I really wish that I could tell you all this without you getting angry with me but you just don't want to talk about Nashville, or the police, or that Mom lost a part of herself while living in that van that we are never going to get back."

Instead, I simply told him it was amazing. I just couldn't find the words.

"Why are you being so vague?"

Well, shit. I was going to have to say something. I had reached the end and I certainly wasn't going to say everything else that was going on in my mind. I wasn't ready for this conversation, because a part of me still held out hope for change. If not in him, at least in the way we communicated with one another. I didn't want our forever relationship to be defined by the angry seventeen-year-old kid in my mind screaming at his father. I wanted to evolve. So, instead of biting remarks or hitting below the belt, I chose to tell my dad about how we got Dole Whip with the 1,000th Happy Haunt.

Halfway through our exhaustingly brilliant day at the Magic Kingdom, we were all highly overheated and in need of a break. We decided to make our way over to the Dole Whip station and try a classic only-at-Disney treat. We ordered both flavors and began our walk towards Frontierland, but as Kira made the turn right in front of Pecos Bill's, she made a slip and in almost slow motion we watched as her pineapple Dole whip flew up in the air and made a masterful splatter on the cement below. Just before someone could cue the sound of Goofy yodeling, a cast member appeared out of nowhere.

He was a large balding man in his mid-fifties wearing all white and a fanny pack while holding a broom and pail. He rushed over next to Kira who had tears glistening in the corners of her eyes, absolutely mortified.

"Would you like to trade pins?"

"I don't have any pins to trade," Kira blurted through sniffles.

"Well, I have an extra pin that is very special. It's Mickey Mouse."

Kira looked up at me for assurance. I smiled at her and at the kindly cast member. He twirled his mustache and smiled back with a cheesy grin pulled straight from the 1950's. It almost seemed familiar, but maybe just cliché. This guy was some kind of character. I couldn't help but be amazed with how even the clean up crew was so full of the magic spirit.

"You know, it all started with a mouse, but this park started with a dad who loved his little girls, just like your daddy loves you."

With that, Kira smiled and hugged the cast member with delight. She then quickly turned to her mother to pin her prized Mickey on her lapel. Just then, he put one finger up in the air as if to remind himself what it is that he was supposed to do. He quickly swept up the mess and tapped Kira on top of her head.

"See, there is no mess we can make that can't be cleaned up. Some people would even say this place was made out of a bunch of failures."

Whatever they paid this guy, it wasn't enough! He should've been in marketing. However, it suddenly became real to all the adults standing there that a Mickey pin wasn't going to be enough. Sadness washed over Kira again as she watched her beautifully mastered sweet treat swept into a waste pail. The cast member looked at me with a reassuring smile.

"Now, Dad, you walk your little Princess right back over there and get her another Dole whip on the house. Tell them that Walt sent you."

I laughed at his joke and then looked at his name badge. It read "WALT." I looked over at Tashina and gave her a little head nod, as if to say,

"Holy crap, this guy's name is really, actually Walt", but when I turned back to face our new friend, he was gone just as quick as he had arrived. Now, I am not saying I believe in ghosts, I am just saying that Walt Disney did. Unfortunately, there is one person who definitely, most assuredly doesn't believe in ghosts, and that is my father.

When I finished telling him the story, he sighed. I couldn't tell if it was just general annoyance or relief that my story was over. After a longer than necessary pause, he said, "It sounds like you guys had a good time with some unique experiences. Hopefully we will all get to go someday, once things get better, you know?"

Maybe Walt was wrong. Maybe not all messes can be turned into Magical Kingdoms.

You've Got a Friend in Me

After listening to the radio for a better part of two hours while Bear slept, I felt relatively certain that he was, in fact, not Charles Manson, because surely they would've announced his escape from prison by now on the show. Either way, I felt a little better about the situation. However, in all honesty, literally almost anything is better than having an escaped Charles Manson in your car, and so my threshold of things being all right was pretty damn low at this point.

He woke up just as we arrived in Pensacola. Now, when I told my parents that I was bringing a friend with me on this trip, I may have failed to mention that my friend was a sixty-year-old homeless Vietnam Veteran with PTSD who resembled a notorious serial killer. Needless to say, I was in a little bit of trouble over the whole thing.

You would think, given their own personal experiences concerning homelessness, they would have been a bit more sympathetic. They awkwardly allowed Bear to have a shower and I believe he spent one night there with us, but after that, I was highly encouraged to take him somewhere else. I dropped Bear off at a local park, "Thanks for the chance kid." And he just turned around and walked off, but it wouldn't be the last time I would see him. During my next visit to Pensacola, he was sitting again in that very same park.

I sat with him for hours and we discussed everything that had happened to him during his visit to the panhandle. It turns out it wasn't the land of milk and honey that I had made it out to be. It seems that he found nothing but the same troubles here as he had in Nashville. No one wanted to hire him, the police harassed him, and there wasn't a lot of help. While I was sitting there talking with him, an older gentleman came up and gave me a $20 dollar bill and told me to go buy my friend something to eat. It seemed like an odd gesture, but I told Bear I would be right back. As I was leaving, I surveyed the park. Bear wasn't the only person who looked like he could use a meal sitting there.

When I returned, I had purchased eighteen or so hamburgers. It turned out that my departure to get food had spread and more people than I had expected were waiting for me. Fortunately, it turned out to be exactly enough hamburgers for everyone. As everyone was sitting around eating, Bear put his arm around my shoulder and pulled me in close to his cigarette stained beard.

"You know kid, this is what we need. Food, and someone who will just listen. You gotta come back next week."

See, what I didn't realize is that all those months ago when Bear asked me if I could spare some change, he wasn't asking if I had money. He wanted someone to see him and listen, someone to sit down and have a meal with him and to be his friend. This time, I wouldn't return back to Nashville and it would finally be of my own free will. It was time to give some change to the poor of Pensacola. The kind of change they were actually asking for.

12. Saving Mr. Banks

"It's kind of fun to do the impossible."
- Walt Disney

The Opening Credits

Once upon a time, there was a man who had two sons and three daughters. He lived in a small village where he was the town musician. Everyone loved to hear him sing and play, especially his children. They lived in a beautiful cottage, where the boys went out to the creek in the mornings to collect berries for their mother, and the girls remained behind to attend to the household. One day, an evil enchantment fell upon the household and the man lost his ability to sing. Without his beautiful voice, the man could no longer support his family. The man decided to go out into the woods behind the cottage to find a way to break the spell, but while he searched, many dangers awaited his family. Sadness crept upon everyone in the house and it became hard to light the fire or find food. Soon, the tax collector of the town came and collected on the mortgage. The children had nowhere to go and because of the shame, the father became cold and distant.

But all spells can be broken if you just believe. And for every evil witch there is a fairy godmother waiting in the wings to turn the mundane into a splendid carriage. Do not be afraid. Though the man had lost his voice and his children, all hope was not lost. This is the story of how the man found his voice, and began to finally sing once again.

If You Just Believe

Fairy tales are true. Every last word. The difference between the lives we live and those of fairy tales is all in how we choose to tell them. No life is truly boring or without adventure. Yes, it is true that in order to tell a compelling story you cannot fill the pages or air with repetitive parts of life that make up the daily rigor, but if you push aside the potty breaks and taco Tuesdays, life is full of beauty, redemption, and magic.

Cinderella had likely given up all hope as she wept, her dress torn and tattered, yet in that very instant, a miracle presented itself. In a similar way, I could have never anticipated the call I received from my father. Nothing spectacular had happened and I knew that things were not well between my parents, but then again life does have a cruel way of waiting to self destruct at the most unlikely times. It would be now—when my father had finally reached a point of financial and career security—that their relationship would reach a true plateau.

The phone rang.

"We have decided to go to Disney World. I know that Tashina will have just had the baby, but if you guys would like to join us … well, we would like to take the whole family."

My heart sank deep into the pit of my stomach. I wanted to go with my family more than anything. My four other siblings were still living at home and even though the new baby would have just arrived, I knew that Tashina would be ecstatic to go back. There was no question how Kira would feel about the subject. But now I was faced with a dilemma, how would I afford to take them?

"I don't want you to have to worry about this, I will be paying for everyone's tickets and we will be renting a house. All I ask is that we can use your van for the trip."

Well, that answered that question. I was still waiting for the other shoe to drop.

Kids have a funny way of accelerating your life. You spent the first twenty-something years of your life waiting to be an adult, and then life starts flashing in blinking moments that soon become distant memories. Things like a wooing a partner, which once seemed like you could write an entire book about that one night, now seems like one second you are making out with your person and the next moment you are doing breathing exercises in the delivery room.

The months leading up to our trip disappeared in the saga of life and parenthood. We welcomed Selena into the family, the latest little princess. On Easter Sunday she was baptized and immediately following the service, my entire family—Mom, Dad, Timothy, Emily, Anna, Aimee, and Tashina, Kira, Selena, and myself—all piled into our respective vehicles. I don't know how it happened, but there it was. Dad sprinkled a little pixie dust, a teary smile appeared on my mothers face, and it was Mom who supplied us with the happy thought. For the first time since we were children, she had found Tootle's marbles. I turned the key and whispered, "Bibbidi Bobbidi Boo." And with that, the cars elevated above the ground, and we looked down at Pensacola below us. We soared high above the clouds and could see Nashville and the small motels and parking lots we once called "home." We soared over the orange trees and the ticking clocks of the crocodiles chasing us, and we left them all behind. It was time for Mr. Darling to put his hook down.

This was our moment.

Just then, Ursula's necklace fell to the ground and released my father's voice. It came rushing through the air to meet us in the sky, and finally for the first time since we were children, my father's voice rang out across the clouds as he sang, "Let's go fly a kite."

And everyone lived happily ever after ... until the next day.

Everything was perfect on our trip. No one fought and everything was happy. For the first time since our childhood, all of my siblings and I were under the same roof at the same time, the bills were paid and the lights weren't going to be shut off. We spent the mornings falling back into familiar routines, pouring cereal and frying eggs. Mom coming behind us and cleaning, shaking her head. Dad would sit with the grandchildren and watch cartoons on the Disney Channel, and then we would run off to a park for a day filled with magic.

We had saved Magic Kingdom for the last day. We would end our family vacation with Walt, the fireworks, and Cinderella's castle. It was going to be the vacation to end all family vacations.

There I was sitting with my dad, watching Indiana Jones dodge a large boulder. He jumped at just the right moments and we smiled and laughed together. In that moment, I was seventeen again, but this time I wasn't angry and Dad was there. To my right, Tashina was planning fast passes on her phone while she nursed the baby, when suddenly she took me by the hand. I know my wife and this wasn't a reassuring thing. This meant something was wrong. I leaned in so she could whisper in my ear.

"Magic Kingdom closes at 7PM tomorrow. There is a special event. We won't be able to see the fireworks."

It had become clear to all of us at some point during our vacation that this trip was bigger than my dad wanting to take us just for the hell of it. At

154

first, Tashina and I speculated that maybe one of my parents was dying. Anna had even pulled me aside expressing that same concern. She thought Dad seemed really skinny and maybe even pale. For the first few days, we watched them like hawks, observing every move. Did Dad just take some medication? Was mom moving slower than usual? After every maneuver had been perfectly scrutinized, we realized that what was dying was my parents. Not physically, but relationally. They had survived hell together, but it seemed that normalcy had become too great a burden after making it through the storm.

We made our exit from the theatre and I pulled Dad aside and gave him the horrific news about the fireworks. Even though my father had spared nearly no expense, he decided not to splurge on the park hopper tickets. Literally the only day we had left to go to see the Magic Kingdom was tomorrow.

My father left the group and said he would go talk with customer service. I offered to go with him.

"No, you wait here. I don't need you blowing your lid on someone. It will just make things worse."

It was the first moment that anyone's former lives or sins had been thrown into our weekend. Everyone had left their weapons at the door and it was a bitter knife to the ribs that I had not expected. I tried to protest, but I could barely find the oxygen. My dad walked off, but a half hour later he returned. There was nothing that could be done, he explained. As minor of a thing as it may have seemed, there was an airy sense of importance about this moment of the entire family standing in the moon shadow of the Castle and seeing the sky light up. I walked away, back in the direction my father had just come from. He grabbed my arm.

"I said there is nothing that can be done."

"Dad, you are going to have to realize someday that I am my own man. I've got to try, because this is my family too."

And with that I walked off.

I walked up to guest services and was greeted with customary smiles and cheer. I thought momentarily that this would be a convenient time for Walt to show back up, but he was nowhere in sight, and so I took my chances with the brunette on the left. I began to explain the entire situation and she smiled less than enthusiastically, "Sir, I understand the situation. Your father was in here a few moments ago. And I appreciate how kind you are being, but there is nothing we can do, and honestly, even if there was something, we aren't generally given to helping people who yell and scream at our cast members."

Why was everyone so dead set on me screaming? I had an absolutely horrific temper during my teen years and I was prone to all kinds of cruelty. Any therapist worth their salt would know that it was simply angst mixed with the toxic combination of genuine trauma and an uncertain home life. However, whenever I was placed in just about any situation at all, my father would bring up my past and shove it right in my face. Everything was prefaced with, "Don't lose your temper," or, "Let's not let things get out of control."

It had become so part of the routine of life that I wondered if there would ever be any redemption for me. It didn't seem to matter how many times I tried hard, or in fact didn't lose my cool, my past would always find me. Now, here I was, thinking I was being great and this woman was regurgitating my father's words of warning back at me.

"But I didn't scream," I protested.

"No, you have been wonderful. Your father, on the other hand, was extremely rude. We had to let our cast member go to break."

Wait one hot minute! My father yelled at someone and I was standing here being all levelheaded and shit. This was amazing. But I couldn't stand here and relish in this moment for much longer. Yes, my father was human and he failed just like me. It seemed my tempter might have been genetic and that somehow my father had just spent years hiding and suppressing it. This was a beautiful moment, but there was a task at hand.

"Listen," I looked at her name tag, just to make sure I wasn't talking to Wendy or Belle, or something, "Rebekah, do you have a minute for me to explain something to you?"

I told her everything. About the house on Liberty Pike with the fleas and about the police. About Aimee being born. We spoke about poverty and how things were going now. I shared with her everything that I have just told you in this book, everything except what happened next, because that had yet to be written, and it all hinged on how she chose to respond in this very moment.

"And so you see, Rebekah, after it is all said and done, I am pretty sure my parents are actually on the verge of getting a divorce. No one has said it, but I think that this might actually be the end. And it just can't be the end. The story can't end this way. I know we don't have a park hopper, and I know that it was posted online that the park would be closed, and somehow we missed all that. But we just have to see those fireworks. There is a lifetime of redemption packed in those explosives and if we don't go tonight, well, that's it. And I have to believe that this is the place where dreams really do come true and so I am wishing on my lucky star that you will have it in you to just see if there is anything at all that can be done."

She gave me a very Mary Poppins look, reached into a bag, and pulled out some tickets, "And how many of you are in your party Mr. Monk?"

She gave us the tickets, but she swore me to secrecy. Under no circumstances was I supposed to tell anyone about this unless it was absolutely necessary, and I have always kept that promise. I hope that you will do the same.

I arrived with those tickets in my hand like I was holding onto one last wish on a lamp. It was a whirlwind as everyone looked at maps and plotted out each move that we needed to make in order for us to round everyone up and make it over to Magic Kingdom in time. A plan was put in place. Tashina was barking orders like a master conductor and off we went, each person playing their part.

That night was spent under the stars and there I stood between my mom and dad with my siblings behind us. There was my beautiful Tashina holding my hand, while the baby nuzzled her chest, and there was my Kira, legs hanging over my shoulders as she looked up in wonder. I looked over at the statue of Walt, who was standing there with us the whole time. Just then, the lights dimmed and Tink flew above the Castle. All of the thousands of beautiful faces from the park that day helped form an image of Walt upon the castle and as he smiled at us all, he said, "To all who come to this happy place, welcome."

As the fireworks lit the sky, they burned up with them all of the negative memories and sadness that had built up to this moment. And as the future would continue to forge forward, new hurts and sadness would take their place, because that is just life. But what we all learned in that moment is that no matter how long it takes, or how hard you have to fight, with a little luck, determination, and with your conscience as your guide, dreams really do come true.

EPILOGUE. UNTIL HAPPILY EVER AFTER

"We believed in our idea - a family park where parents and children could have fun- together."
- Walt Disney

Life is far too nuanced to fit into one book and I am certain if I tried it would likely make me go as mad as a hatter. As I attempted to pen these pages, I wrestled greatly with how much detail I should supply. Should I write about the smell of the motel rooms or the stained sheets? Should I make clear, in exhausting terms, exactly how many nights we spent homeless? What does that add or subtract from the reality of our situation? In this collection of stories, I have instead attempted, to the best that I am able, to explain how it felt, and which things felt important to me as a child and now as an adult.

Within the true story of my life individually, and also within my life as part of a family, there has been fault on every person to some extent that has led to hurt and pain. It would be profoundly unfair for me to lay all of that burden at the feet of my father or my mother. There is also society to blame for so much of what has happened, the stigma that comes with homelessness, and the arrogant ways in which certain agencies or religious groups attempt to address it, placing themselves at some higher vantage point.

We have all played our part in the great circle of life, but I also do not believe that any person should be defined by their time without a home. One of the great frustrations I have felt both while living within the world of being homeless, and also as an advocate for those who are currently suffering at the hands of poverty, is that homelessness seems to act like a prison tattoo that can never be removed. And if you aren't careful that ink can bleed straight into your soul, forever staining you.

These stories do not define my parents, my siblings, myself, or any other person mentioned in these pages. I would imagine, as you read these words, that portions of them resonated with you. Perhaps they feel familiar to experiences very similar to your own, regardless of your station in life. What you are feeling in that kindred moment is the universal bond of humanity. That is all this book is—a highlight of the human experience within a finite period of time, nothing more or less. Maybe your great adventure is not Disney World. It could be climbing Everest, taking your children to a baseball game, or devoting yourself to silent reflection in monastic life. Common ground is found not in what we dream about, but in the human ability to have dreams and seek after them.

There exists, now more than ever, an undercurrent to dehumanize the poor and homeless, as if they are some form of "other" than the rest of the population. However, I can attest as someone who has been homeless, that I was not something other than you, nor was I something other than I am now. I was simply a person going through an experience, and the length of time or cause that brought us to that point of living without does not change anything about my humanity.

So, should I tell you where everyone is now? If I did so, would that further humanize my family and endear us to the reader in such a way that they could relate even more? I could literally begin to write out the current happy endings of those listed in this book and before I receive it back from the printer, everything could change. However, that change, if it were to occur, would change nothing about the humanity of those individuals. Likewise, someone's story should not have to be touching in order for him or her to deserve help.

Beautiful stories exist everywhere. We read about them all the time. A homeless man who can play piano and almost finished college before life got in the way. Then we hear about how his music inspired someone, scholarships are offered, and he gets back on track. However, for every single story that exists like this, there are also countless stories of those who are so crippled by mental illness and years of self-medication, that the thought of sobriety seems nearly impossible and arguably inhumane to suggest. Does this person's life deserve less dignity because their addiction has been so strong that they are unable to overcome it? Perhaps, more likely, the system has been so failed they were never given the chance to succeed.

I would argue that as a society we are judged far more by how we treat the cases that are harder to handle, than by those personal empowerment pieces that are easier to put on fundraising brochures.

It is here that I would argue that no family or individual is worthy of being considered the success case, at least not anymore than someone deserves to be considered a failure or lost cause. Life does not fit into as neat of a box as I have even portrayed in this very book you are reading. My father and I still fight from time to time, though certainly less than before. That being said, he has yet to read this book and so it is quite possible that shortly you will find me writing a sequel entitled, "Chasing ... Me Out of Town."

What I hope you take away from this disfigured rendering of my experience is the gut wrenching reality of our family's humanity and that it is no different than your own. That the love for my siblings that I share with you here, I also share with you in reality.

What I have spoken about here is genuine. The struggles of those whom you have now become endeared to within these chapters are real people I have met and also loved. Many of them have since died or succumbed so deep into addiction that they are unrecognizable. Others have gone on to live productive, yet completely flawed lives. There are countless others whom I will never know the outcome simply because they have disappeared into the night, maybe to appear again someday.

This is not my life story. This is the story of a moment of my life and how some of those moments have connected to other events, shaping me into the person I am today. Just as these events have shaped me, they were also shaping others as well. Were my father to sit down and write this very same book, his perspective would be highly different and come with many vantages I was not afforded in my childhood.

By design, I did not discuss these things with my parents as I wrote this book. It was important for me to capture—as best as I could—the raw feelings that lay upon the surface. I could have easily sat my parents down and timelined everything, making sure I remained accurate to both their truth and my own. Had I done that, I fear, I would have lost a very important element to this story, and that is the unchecked feelings of a sometimes confused, sometimes angry child who experienced something very difficult.

What you do with these pages is up to you. My only hope is that you do something with this information. If it has helped affirm what you already knew, then I hope that you will be reinvigorated to fight against injustice wherever you see it. If this information is somehow new to you, I challenge you to seek out answers and to forge relationships with people like Bear, who taught me so very much.

When this is all said and done, whatever you do, please see each other. That is absolutely the most important part and the lesson I have learned so profoundly during this experience. If you are willing to take the time, to sit down with people different than yourself and break bread with them, you will find a common ground, even if all that might be is the great human connector, the ability to dream for the impossible.

About the Author:

Nathan Monk is a civil rights activist, author, and former Orthodox priest. He resides in Pensacola, FL with his partner Tashina and together they are the parents of three children, Kira, Selena, and Gideon. Though he is best known for his social activism, he has been frequently spotted frolicking with woodland creatures.

For more than a decade, Nathan has worked tirelessly for social justice, specifically for the homeless.

Nathan holds a Masters Degree in Theology and served as a priest for eight years before resigning in 2013 after stepping out in support of marriage equality. He was subsequently declared de facto excommunicated and defrocked by the hierarchy of the Church, though the Church fell short of formally processing any official declarations of laicization.

Currently, he is the executive director of a non-profit focused on housing solutions for homeless families.

Over his career, he has received notable awards, appointments, and national media for his accomplishments in the area of social justice. He was appointed by Mayor Ashton Hayward III as the co-chair of the Task Force on Human Services, a focus group tasked with finding practical solutions to address homelessness and poverty. The Pensacola City Council appointed him to the City Planning Board. He received international recognition for helping fight to overturn the city's notorious "blanket ban" which made it illegal for the homeless to utilize any device to shield themselves from the elements.

Nathan Monk is active on
social media…

Follow
@FatherNathan

to get updates.

facebook.com/FatherNathan

twitter.com/FatherNathan

instagram.com/FatherNathan

www.TinyHouseBigSolution.com

www.FatherNathanMonk.com

96377586R00107

Made in the USA
Columbia, SC
28 May 2018